There are plenty of management theories available from people who have never managed anything bigger than a corner grocery. Here the billionaire businessman whom *Fortune* calls "the richest man in the world" tells what he has learned from building and managing some of the most successful enterprises in his career. And what he has learned from his mistakes as well!

Also by J. Paul Getty
from Jove

HOW TO BE RICH

J.PAUL GETTY

HOW TO BE A SUCCESSFUL EXECUTIVE

A JOVE BOOK

Portions of this book have appeared
in *Playboy* magazine.

HOW TO BE A SUCCESSFUL EXECUTIVE

A Jove Book / published by arrangement with
Playboy Press

PRINTING HISTORY
Playboy Press hardcover edition / published 1971
Playboy Press softcover edition / published 1972
Jove edition / November 1984

ISBN: 0-515-07912-X

Jove books are published by The Berkley Publishing Group,
200 Madison Avenue, New York, N.Y. 10016.
The words "A JOVE BOOK" and the "J" with sunburst
are trademarks belonging to Jove Publications, Inc.

PRINTED IN THE UNITED STATES OF AMERICA

CONTENTS

1.
BUSINESS IS BUSINESS

**THE FIELDS OF ENDEAVOR MAY VARY,
BUT THE GROUND RULES
FOR FISCAL SUCCESS
REMAIN THE SAME**

Shortly after the United States entered World War Two, I tried to obtain a commission in the U.S. Navy. On February 20, 1942, I had an interview in Washington, D.C., with Colonel Frank Knox, who was then the secretary of the navy.

Colonel Knox, aware that I indirectly held a controlling interest in the Spartan Aircraft Corporation and the Spartan Aeronautical School, urged me to abandon my plans. Instead, he asked me to take over active personal management of these companies.

"That would be the most useful thing you could do for the navy and for your country," he told me. "We need aircraft and airplane parts—and trained fliers—desperately. To obtain them, we must have experienced businessmen running our plants and flying schools—men who can rapidly expand manufacturing and training facilities and raise production to unprecedented levels."

Two days later, I was in Tulsa, Oklahoma, where Spartan Aircraft and the Spartan Aeronautical School were located. The former was a small company that had been established in 1928. The latter, a thriving training plant turning out air and ground crews for the U.S. and Allied air forces, was already well on its way to becoming the largest privately owned flying school in the country. It was being well managed by Captain Max Balfour, a veteran pilot and top-notch administrator. The factory, still geared for post-Depression civilian production, needed much attention.

Now, my knowledge of airplane manufacture was nil. I knew little more about airplanes than that they had wings and engines and that if they were properly built and piloted, they flew. My business career up to that time had been largely devoted to finding, producing, refining and marketing oil. Admittedly, I'd made some tangential essays into other fields, including real estate and even the hotel business, but I certainly had no experience even remotely related to the manufacture of airplanes. On February 21, 1942, while en route from Washington to Tulsa, I made the following notation in my diary: "I have an important job—getting the Spartan factory into mass production for the army and navy."

I faced this job with no small degree of trepidation. It was no normal peacetime venture. The factory would not be producing everyday items for civilian use. Its products would be highly im-

9

portant—possibly even vital—to the nation's war effort. Airplanes were not porch swings or doorknobs; they were fantastically complex machines whose components had to be manufactured with infinite precision. There could be no margin of error; any mistake or miscalculation would cost human lives.

Could I handle the job? I'd asked myself this question a thousand times in the two days that followed my interview with Secretary Knox. Upon my arrival in Tulsa, I made an intensive inspection of the Spartan plant, studied the company's books and records and conferred at length with the firm's executives and employees. Within 48 hours, I had the answer to my question. My job was to "expand manufacturing and training facilities" at Spartan, to boost the production of airplanes and the number of trained men to fly and service them. I felt certain I could do it.

It seemed logical to me that the basic principles involved in accomplishing these tasks would be the same as those involved in, say, the expansion of an oil company. Granted, there would be vast differences in the technical aspects. One does not drill an engine-mount bracket to a one-thousandth-of-an-inch tolerance in precisely the same way one drills a mile-deep oil well. When one builds a storage shed, he can, in a pinch, substitute asbestos roofing for galvanized iron; but there can be no substitutions when, for example, specifications for a wing surface call for a certain gauge and type of aluminum alloy. I also knew that time was very short and materials scarce and that labor would have to be recruited and trained. But I'd had experience with fairly analogous situations previously in my career, particularly in the great oil-boom periods in Oklahoma and California.

In short, I reasoned that business is business—whatever type of business it may be. And, according to my definition, "doing business" is nothing more nor less than performing a service that has a commercial value.

Of course, in the case of Spartan, the service that the company—and I—had to perform was not commercial in the most widely accepted sense of the word. The primary aim was not to build the company or to make profits but to do everything humanly possible to help win the war. Nonetheless, the service could be considered commercial in the sense that Spartan had to turn out top-quality products at maximum speed and at the lowest possible prices in order to meet a huge and exigent demand.

Once I viewed my new job in this light, the problems of getting Spartan's operations into high gear diminished to entirely manageable proportions. I realized that I need only apply the same principles that I had always used in business. I soon found that these were just as valid when applied to airplane manufacture as they had been when I'd applied them to my oil business.

Before long, army and navy representatives were accepting my forecasts of time needed to get various items into production and my estimates of ultimate output, considering them more reliable than predictions contained in surveys made by various "efficiency experts."

In one instance—in April 1942—Spartan received a subcontract to manufacture wings for the navy's Grumman fighter planes. The experts predicted that it would take the factory at least 15 months to tool up, train labor and get into full production on the wings. They backed their prediction with the customary Everests of charts, tables and graphs. At this time, the war situation was anything but bright. The Philippines had fallen; the Nazis continued their advance into Russia. The U.S. and its allies were on the defensive everywhere, while the Axis powers were celebrating triumphs large and small on all fronts. Under these circumstances, 15 months seemed an unconscionably long time to get into production on wings for urgently needed fighter aircraft.

I wasn't overly impressed by the forecasts of the factory experts. I've often found that the trouble with many experts is that they're technicians, not businessmen; they frequently seem to lack the built-in enterprise and competitive spirit that motivate businessmen to beat deadlines and achieve results quickly. I· talked the matter over with Spartan executives, supervisory personnel and line workers. All of them recognized the challenge and the need for speed. We slashed the time-lag estimate down to six months. Needless to say, the experts howled their protests and disbelief.

"Paul Getty has never run an aircraft plant before in his life!" they chorused. "He doesn't know what he's doing!"

Although Grumman and navy representatives were somewhat skeptical about Spartan's ability to begin deliveries within six months, they agreed to go along with my estimates and to cooperate in every way possible. My production chief and I promptly selected 50 of our best workers and shipped them off to the prime contractor's plant in

California. There they were given intensive on-the-job training in the most efficient methods of producing wings for the firm's fighter planes. In the meantime, we began tooling up feverishly at Spartan. We had ten jigs ready by the time the men returned to Tulsa. Spartan was in production on the Grumman subcontract in slightly less than the six months I'd estimated. What's more, Spartan workers reduced production time from a normal 400 hours per unit to an astounding 40 hours per unit.

By the time I had been at Spartan two years, I had ample reason to feel proud of the company's achievements and of its contribution to the war effort. Factory floor space had been increased from some 65,000 square feet to more than 300,000. The plant, which had formerly employed only a handful of people, now had over 5500 employees—loyal, hardworking men and women who certainly earned the efficiency awards the company received from the United States Government. By February 14, 1944, I could note in my diary that Spartan had produced 90 training planes on prime contract, 155 sets of wings for Grumman fighters, 650 Curtiss dive-bomber cowlings, all the control surfaces for 1100 Douglas dive bombers, 5800 sets of elevators, ailerons and rudders for B-24 bombers, and a great quantity of other aircraft components and subassemblies.

The point of all this? Business is business. Business principles do not change; the fundamentals remain constant no matter what the field or industry involved.

When I began my career more than 50 years ago, it was assumed that if an individual was a

13

businessman, he could handle almost any type of business. It was hardly considered unusual for a man to own a mill, a department store, a brace of office buildings and perhaps even a bank—and make a success of running them all. It was taken for granted that a man who possessed the necessary traits of leadership, imagination, ambition and enterprise—who "had a good business head on his shoulders"—could operate almost any form of commercial endeavor. I am well aware that business is far more complex now than it was then. Nevertheless, I still think it can be done and that there are still men who can do it.

Don't misunderstand me. In no way am I trying to imply that I think that businessmen are born and not made. I'd be the last person in the world to advance any such theory, for I have my own example and experience to indicate that the opposite is probably true. I most certainly was not a born businessman. Quite to the contrary. I showed no early urge or drive—or, for that matter, talent —to be a businessman. My own thirst for lemonade quickly doomed my juvenile forays into lemonade-stand operation. I had only indifferent success as a magazine-subscription salesman. I suppose the closest I came to having any childhood feel for business was the strong feeling of competitiveness I derived from being an avid collector and trader of marbles and automobile catalogs, two items dearly prized by most boys in those days.

As a young man, I wanted to join the United States diplomatic service and to be a writer. I most probably would have tried to realize these ambitions, even after I'd achieved my first successes as a wildcatter in Oklahoma, had I not been an only child.

My father, George F. Getty, devoted his entire life to building his business. If I'd had a brother or brothers who could have taken over from him, I doubtless would have become a diplomat or a writer. As it was, I had no brothers, but I did have a sense of responsibility toward my father, his employees and the shareholders in his companies. It was a sense of duty to them that impelled me to abandon my ambitions and enter the family business. However, once I did decide to go into business, I determined to be a businessman of the kind that William H. Whyte calls an entrepreneur, rather than the organization-man type he labels a collaborator, who is merely a cog that spins in the business machine only because the big gears are turning.

My formal education had been mainly in the humanities. My practical training had been in the oil fields, where I'd worked as a roustabout and tool-dresser. Thus, I had much to learn about business, and, more often than not, the lessons were anything but easy. But learn I did—most particularly, the basic truth I've already stated, that the principles of business apply with equal force and validity to all forms of commercial enterprise. And, in my opinion, one of the most important of these principles is implied in the definition of business as "performing a service that has a commercial value."

Plainly, a business must supply a need. In so doing, it must give value for value received. The value received—or the price of the service rendered or product sold—must be fair, low enough to be within the buyer's ability to pay, yet high enough to give the business a reasonable profit.

In order to keep old customers, obtain new ones, meet competition and justify his profits, the businessman must constantly seek to raise quality, reduce costs (and prices), increase production and improve all facets of his business. He must accept the facts that he will always be faced with problems and that these exist only to be solved in the most efficient manner possible. Once he accepts these concepts, he must train himself to be an imaginative innovator, able to meet any situation by applying his cumulative knowledge and experience to whatever new obstacles confront him.

Actually, there are very few unique business problems or situations. Anyone in business for any length of time soon realizes that there are, within the realm of his own experience, precedents to almost any problem that may arise. A drilling rig and an airframe may not seem to have much in common, but the construction of one is analogous to the construction of the other, if only because both must be built from raw materials to perform certain tasks. Lessons learned in eliminating delays and bottlenecks in the construction of one can, if applied imaginatively, go a long way toward showing how similar problems may be solved in the construction of the other. Even my experience in hotel operation and construction proved invaluable when it became necessary to build housing accommodations—and eventually a miniature city—for Getty Oil Company employees in our Middle Eastern oil fields.

I could cite countless other examples to show how previous business knowledge and experience may be applied imaginatively to new and different business situations. However, I believe it is more important to emphasize that experience *alone* is hardly enough to make an individual a successful all-around businessman. Mere experience, without the imagination to use it constructively and creatively and without business ability, is likely to be more handicap than advantage. There are many men for whom experience serves as a mental straitjacket. They are unable to apply imaginatively what they already know; they only repeat what they first learned. The experience of five, ten or twenty years actually stultifies such men. Instead of adapting what they know to new situations, they try to make all new situations conform to patterns with which they are familiar.

As for "business ability," this is something of an imponderable, comprised of many ingredients. Among these are large measures of common sense, ambition, versatility, a highly developed spirit of competitiveness, a genuine interest in business, a healthy appetite for the give-and-take of the marketplace, resourcefulness—and an ingrained understanding of the concept that business is performing a service that has a commercial value.

I have said that I was not a born businessman. But, as I have also said, when I did go into business, it was with the determination to be an entrepreneur. To my way of thinking, being in business was worthwhile and challenging only if one viewed it as a form of creative work. My career has seasoned me as a businessman and has taught me not only that business is business but that there are commercial possibilities in almost everything. To me, an empty lot is not just an empty lot—it is a potential site for a house, a store or a filling station. If I went to a remote Greek island inhabited by poor fishermen and farmers, I would automatically start looking for natural resources that could be developed or for industries that could be established on the island. True, the profit motive would be present, but profits could come only after the life of the islanders had been bettered by putting their human energy to more productive use.

The farsighted businessman realizes that he can render the greatest commercial service by taking advantage of every opportunity. And there are opportunities everywhere for creating new businesses, even entire new industries, and for building and expanding old ones. They exist in profusion on remote Greek islands, in developed countries and underdeveloped ones—and in our own backyards.

It is often charged that the modern-day business executive is too much of a specialist and not enough of a businessman. I'm forced to agree that there is more than a grain of truth to this. Overspecialization has narrowed the outlooks of some of our most promising men.

On the other hand, it must also be admitted that the present-day business executive is a better businessman than the old-timer, in the same way that the modern physician is a better doctor than was the GP of a few decades ago.

Both the doctor and the executive of today are specialists. Both have had intensive training in their specialties, and both have more and better tools with which to work. The modern heart specialist has the electrocardiograph and other scientific instruments to aid his diagnosis. The GP had to rely on his stethoscope, the patient's symptoms, diagnostic questioning—and his own experience and intuition. The oil prospector of today is aided by seismographic tests, vast quantities of geologists' data and other technical devices and information. The oil prospector of 1917, by contrast, had to feel and guess his way to oil.

To such extents as these, doctors and business executives are today more efficient and less liable to make errors—in their own specialized fields. But I wonder if the average heart specialist can deliver a baby, set a broken arm or remove an appendix as well as the old-time GP. I certainly know innumerable executives who are specialized in highly restricted fields but who are completely lost when asked to take over a department other than their own.

While the modern technician-executive may know far more about one particular aspect of business than does the all-around businessman, the latter's grasp of the whole and all its parts is much greater. And, consequently, it is the all-around businessman—the entrepreneur—who has the best chance of reaching the top. As one extremely successful businessman remarked to me recently: "I own several businesses and I run them all profitably. If I get stuck and need a specialist, I can always put one on the payroll, but I can't hire anyone to do my job. The men who could handle it are in business for themselves, making their own fortunes."

In my opinion, modern business has a great need for more entrepreneurs. I believe there is more opportunity for a young man to become a successful entrepreneur today than ever before, if only because specimens of the breed are fewer and farther between.

How to do it? First of all, an individual must possess business ability, imagination and enterprise. He must be of the type who would rather run the show than be a supporting player. He should conceive of business as a form of creative effort and understand that business principles are the same whether one is manufacturing safety pins or skyscrapers.

His education should be as broad as possible. Whether obtained at a university or in the college of hard knocks—and preferably in a combination of the two—it should give him a multidimensional background and outlook. A highly specialized education is fine—for the specialist. But the wider the scope of the entrepreneur's education, the more capable he is of grasping the problems he will have to face.

Then, no matter what field he enters initially, he must learn as much as he can about all aspects of it. In short, he must be a sort of GP of business —versed in everything from accounting to warehousing—to the extent that he can direct every facet of the business.

Lastly, and perhaps more importantly, the would-be entrepreneur must have it clearly in mind that business is business. The entrepreneur who knows one business thoroughly can operate another—or a dozen others—as handily as the first.

There's a great challenge and a great satisfaction in being an entrepreneur in the business world. It's fun, and it's highly profitable. It's also the shortest, fastest and surest road to success.

2.
HOW
I WOULD START
AGAIN TODAY

INDUSTRY'S ELYSIAN FIELDS—
CURRENT AND FUTURE—
AWAIT THE YOUNG MAN
ABOUT TO EMBARK ON A CAREER
OR LAUNCH A BUSINESS OF HIS OWN

A few months ago, I was interviewed by a correspondent for a European business publication. After asking a great many questions about my business career, he paused, shook his head sadly and declared, "It is a pity your countrymen of today do not enjoy the same opportunities to achieve success as were present when you started in business."

I'm afraid I reacted rather violently, for, as I told the journalist, there is more opportunity for the beginner in business today than ever before in our history. I cited individuals and companies, facts and figures that prove conclusively that the day of the remarkable business success story is still very much with us. I held forth at length, and

I think I made my point; the correspondent departed visibly impressed and, I believe, convinced.

There are far too many people who labor under the same misapprehension: that our present day offers diminished opportunity for the businessman, particularly for the beginner.

Back in 1958, in a magazine article entitled *You Can Make a Million*, which was directed at an audience of men in the 21-to-40 age group, I wrote, "I envy your chances. I wish I could take them for you. It would be fun to do it all over again."

My opinions have certainly not changed since. Quite the contrary—the dizzying speed of technological progress during the intervening years has served to make me even more enthusiastic about the prospects facing anyone who starts a business career today, whether as an investor or as an employed executive.

A fabulous business landscape spreads literally into infinity before the eyes of the imaginative beginner. It is a landscape rich in opportunity, richer by far than even those that unfolded during the golden eras of the Industrial Revolution, the American expansion and the postwar boom.

Charles Bates ("Tex") Thornton, the fireball chairman of Litton Industries—whose personal success story, incidentally, is a classic of our present time—dramatically stated the promise of the future when he said, "During the next ten years, there should be more scientific and technological advancement than in all history, more than double that of the past twenty years. There's really no place to stop. We will never reach our destination."

TEMPO—Technical Military Planning Operation—one of the nation's most respected scientific organizations, makes the following glowing prediction: "America and the world will change over the next dozen years at a quickening pace, faster than that of the past two decades." And, prophesies TEMPO, U.S. industrial production will practically double, the average family income will be near $10,000 annually, and the gross national product will be close to a *trillion* dollars.

I do not think it necessary to dwell here on the fact that, in the last two decades, innumerable Americans and American companies have earned well-deserved fortunes in a variety of fields ranging from packaging to chemicals to electronics and beyond. I would presume that this fact is sufficiently familiar to the readers of this book.

The important thing, as Tex Thornton, TEMPO and other knowledgeable sources predict—and as farsighted businessmen agree—is that the surface has barely been scratched. The biggest leaps forward—U.S. free-enterprise style, I hasten to make clear, and *not* the Red Chinese variety—and the most tempting plums lie ahead.

Since the overall business trend is *up*, with burgeoning populations, enlightened economic policies and other factors pointing to continuing expansion and growth, there is a fine future for the tyro in most areas. However, the ambitious beginner is especially likely to achieve success along two different but interconnected avenues. Both are equally broad, challenging and open— and equally liable to be paved with gold.

Which of them the beginner chooses to take is a decision he must make himself. Much depends on such elements as personal interest and aptitude.

However, each offers enormous promise, and I propose to examine both in detail.

The first avenue to success for the beginner is offered by those older, what might be called traditional, industries that are undergoing, or that will soon undergo, revolutionary changes that will completely transform their character. An example that comes immediately to mind is the transportation industry. The revolution in transportation has been under way for thousands of years, but since the turn of the century its pace has been accelerated at a fantastic rate. Supertankers, jet aircraft, "ground-effect machines"—such as the "hovercraft" and "aircars"—hydrofoil vessels and superspeed monorails are already with us. So are giant pipelines that carry petroleum products, wood pulp, coal slurry, sulfur, sugarcane and many other fluids and semisolids.

Great submarine cargo vessels and huge plastic "sausages" that can be filled with cargo and towed underwater, transcontinental pipeline networks to transport coal and perhaps other solid commodities, cross-country conveyors to carry goods, and crosstown moving-sidewalk conveyors to carry people—all these and more are within sight. Such practical-minded and generally reliable prognosticators as RCA's David Sarnoff are predicting the advent of pilotless, completely automated and rocket-propelled passenger transports. And then, of course, there is space travel. . . .

But, even as his imagination boggles at the picture of the transportation industry of the near future, the imaginative young businessman can readily grasp the potentials and possibilities offered by this revolution in moving things and people. It doesn't matter how he wants to get in on the ground floor, by offering his talents as an executive or by supplying his capital as an investor.

All these radical changes will require men with fresh, flexible minds. Naturally, engineers will be in great demand. But so will accountants, purchasing executives and sales executives—and plain all-around managers—whose minds and reflexes are such as to permit them to move easily into a traditional industry that will soon become unrecognizable.

The materials industries provide another example of an area of business and industrial activity that is in the process of metamorphosis. Dr. Lee DuBridge has coined the expression *molecular engineering* to describe the technology of changing the characteristics of materials. Tremendous strides have already been made in this direction. Unnumbered new synthetics, alloys and combinations of materials have appeared on the market for use in everything from children's clothing to space rockets.

Such progress will continue at an ever-increasing pace during the coming years. New materials will be developed in laboratories and produced for the world's increasingly materials-hungry markets. Nonetheless, I anticipate that the majority of traditional materials will hold their own or even do better than ever before. Science and technology will devise ways to improve traditional materials, combine them with other materials for better results and find new uses and applications for them. In short, the materials field is definitely one that will see radical changes, and it is also a fertile field for the fledgling businessman who hopes to achieve an early success.

"It is hard to think of an industrial or consumer product that will not be made stronger, lighter, cheaper, more attractive or more durable by taking advantage of new materials," James R. Bright wrote in a recent *Harvard Business Review* article.

That statement alone should tell the whole story in a nutshell to the perceptive tyro. It reflects the basic truth that the materials field is wide open for the man of vision and ability. I feel that it will be even more so in the future, as the world embarks on vast construction projects of all kinds and continues to expand its industries to meet the spiraling demand for products of every sort.

The technologist and engineer will find much opportunity in the materials field. The same holds for the sales and sales-promotion executive. And it also holds for the man who sits in the home office and, as James Bright puts it, understands "the economics and technicalities of the customers' manufacturing processes and applications of their own products vis-à-vis competitive materials." But materials industries are no different from any other in the sense that, as they change and grow, they will need capable executives of every type, and they will also need distributors, jobbers and dealers. All in all, the enterprising beginning businessman will find ample scope in the materials area.

There are many other traditional industries that are undergoing top-to-bottom transformations. In general, what applies to the two examples I have cited—transportation and materials—applies to these as well. The period of transition, in which the old is phased out and the new is phased in, is an ideal time for the beginner. Acquainted with the old but not hidebound by it, he is also fresh

27

and adaptable enough to grasp the new and to make the most of the changing developments around him.

Now I would like to discuss the second avenue to success that, I believe, offers particular promise to the beginner. It is represented by the completely new industries that have recently emerged—and will continue to emerge in large numbers in the future—as a result of major scientific and technological breakthroughs. These offer broad opportunities and, to the individual about to start his business career, they are doubtless invested with an extra glamour—as well they might be, for it is in these areas that our economy has its most challenging frontiers.

Energy is one of the most important of these areas. At present, oil, coal, gas and hydroelectric power are still the world's principal energy sources, though the picture began to change when the development of the A-bomb opened the door to the utilization of atomic power.

The potentials of nuclear energy are fairly well known. There are already nuclear reactors producing power for peaceful purposes; there can be no doubt that we shall see a progressively wider application of this energy source in the years ahead. Only a short time ago, newspapers reported that, at least in theory, every home in the nation could one day be heated by nuclear-fueled heating systems. In 1963, the U.S. Navy requested authorization to power *all* its fighting craft of more than 8000 tons with nuclear energy.

David Sarnoff says, "I do not hesitate to forecast

that atomic batteries will be commonplace long before 1980."

Scientists are also studying and developing means to harness other hitherto-untapped sources of energy. Solar energy is one example. Steady progress is being made in research to find more efficient and economical ways to store the free, and theoretically limitless, energy of the sun's rays. Efforts are also being made to harness the enormous energy expended by ocean tides.

Temperatures running into the tens of millions of degrees have already been achieved in the laboratory by physicists working in a field called magnetohydrodynamics, or plasma physics. This involves the handling of extremely hot gases in magnetic fields, and its goal is to tap the fantastic power of hydrogen fusion.

These and other studies aimed at finding new sources of energy are proceeding apace. I'm inclined to believe there will be many startling breakthroughs in this area within the next decade or so. Incidentally, although I am principally in the oil business and such developments might possibly downgrade the importance of oil as an energy source, I am not worried. Science has proved— and experience has shown—that oil, like coal, possesses properties that make it particularly suited for use as a raw material in organic chemical synthesis. Chemists, physicists and engineers will find endless new uses for oil, producing from it a whole spectrum of wonder products. In this respect, I feel that oil still has a very long way to go before coming of age, but I also feel that the distant goal will be reached in a comparatively short time.

Withal, the new energy industries will offer the beginning businessman myriad opportunities for resounding success. And do not think for a moment that these will be limited to technicians. As just one off-the-cuff observation—which should serve to spark the imagination—think of what will happen when the atomic battery is perfected and placed on the market. Aside from all the investment that will be needed to produce and distribute the batteries, armies of crack executives will be needed to manage this new industry. And fortunes will be made by the individuals and companies who plan and implement the programs to convince an understandably atom-shy public that the new product will not make a Hiroshima out of Hartford or Hoboken.

Electronics—although it has taken astounding giant steps in recent years—is also still in its infancy. Here is another new industry that will continue renewing itself during the career span of any young man now embarking on business life. There are no bounds to the uses to which electronic equipment might be put. Computer development will make all that is familiar now seem as antiquated as the hand-operated adding machine. As far back as 1955, David Sarnoff, in his book *In the Fabulous Future: America in 1980*, predicted tubeless television and electronic light. Arthur C. Clarke's book *Profiles of the Future* predicts that "within a few years our present [communications] facilities [will] seem as primitive as Indian smoke signals." Tex Thornton foresees the time when there will be absolutely no need for anyone to carry money or checks; a purchaser will need only to hold up his thumb before an electronic scanning device. At lightning speed, the device will check his *bona fides* and automatically subtract the amount due from his bank account.

I could go on indefinitely, listing the electronic marvels that are even now under development— and some of which might well be on the market by the time this book is in print, such is the awesome speed of our progress. However, to extend the list would be unnecessary. The fledgling businessman worth the name will see the fantastic promise of electronics. The beginner can get his big chance in research, development, production, sales and distribution or servicing, in any phase of the mushrooming industry.

Breadth of opportunity and open doors in virtually all departments are characteristics of the new industries. Even those that start from scratch show such immense potential that there is hardly a managerial field that will not require hosts of new men. Desalinization, for instance, gives much promise of one day becoming an important industry. The population explosion and centuries of deforestation have made fresh, sweet water less available in many areas, a serious problem in others. More and more water will be needed for human and industrial use, for irrigation and for the reclamation of arid regions in an increasingly crowded world. The desalinization of seawater offers a theoretically feasible answer to this problem. The main problem now, as I understand it, is to devise a process that will desalinate the requisite vast quantities of ocean water fast enough and economically enough to permit widespread use.

Science is working on this right now. The breakthrough is bound to come, and when it does, there will be opportunities galore for the beginner. Not only will there be fine executive openings in what is certain to become a large industry virtually over-night, but there will be golden harvests for those who understand the implications and move in to develop lands that had previously been worthless but that will be extremely valuable as the new water supplies become available. And this is only one of many by-products the economical desalinization of ocean water will offer astute businessmen.

The space industries have awesome potential. True, they are now working almost exclusively on government contracts, and they may well continue to do so, for the capital expenditures needed seem far beyond the capacity of any private company or even any private consortium. However, the companies that produce the equipment for the space program are largely private firms, operating under the free-enterprise system, and all signs indicate they will continue to do so.

For the beginner in the space industries, the stars are the limit. The human animal being what he is, he will not rest but will continue to move ahead from one unknown to another. It is no more possible to reverse or halt man's exploration of space than it was to halt the global exploration that began in the 15th Century.

Space programs will expand. Those who complain about the cost might do well to remember that Queen Isabella was—at least according to legend—forced to give up her jewels in order to finance Columbus's expedition. History often repeats itself by offering recurrent parallels, and I believe that the eventual rewards of space exploration will be proportionately as great as those ultimately reaped from the voyage of Columbus.

The enterprising would-be businessman whose

interests and aptitudes lie in that direction will not hesitate to leap aboard the space-industry bandwagon. Just as in the other industries and areas that I have listed, he will find more than ample latitude to prove his abilities, whether he enters this field as an executive or as an investor.

I have not covered all the new industries. It would take far more space than I have here to mention them. Lasers, ultrasonics, pantography, thermionics, the retardation prevention of organic deterioration (irradiation, freezing, dehydration) are only some of the many areas that space limitations prevent me from discussing. However, if I were starting out on my business career today, I would certainly make a careful assessment of the possibilities offered by each of the industries and fields I have mentioned—as well, I might suggest, as those I have omitted.

As I have previously suggested, my final decision would be governed to no small extent by another assessment—that of my own abilities and inclinations. There is less and less chance for the square peg to squeeze himself into the round hole under today's complex, fast-moving conditions; a man who doesn't know and cannot learn what he is doing and is not comfortable in his work hasn't much chance of getting off the ground, much less to the top.

Before a beginner can begin, his biggest job is that of appraising, not praising, himself. He must carefully weigh his strong points and his weak points. If he has the capital to invest in some business, then he must proceed with care—care for himself and his money. I know that it sounds childish to say that the investor should know, or have a very good idea of, what he is doing. But, childish as it sounds, too many individuals invest their money subjectively, on a whim, in a burst of enthusiasm or on the advice of some fast-talking pitchman. It is necessary to learn as much as is humanly possible about any venture before investing in it. That dictum has held good through the ages; it will continue to hold good in the future. No scientific or technological advancement will change it.

As for the individual just graduating from college or completing a postgraduate course—one who wants to work his way up the ladder or to gain experience before going into business for himself—my advice is also, on the face of it, too simple: He should get a good job with a good company in the field of his considered choice.

It is essential to bear in mind that in a large company, the executive tends to learn and experience only one phase, or at best only a few phases, of business operations. In a small company, on the other hand, he is much more likely to learn about the overall operation of the business and thus has more chance of developing into a seasoned, all-around manager and businessman.

As for going into business for himself, the employed executive must be certain that he is ready for the big step, ready to graduate from the payroll to the position of the man who has to meet it. He must feel that he has sufficient experience, and sufficient aptitude and acumen, for doing business on his own profitably. Nothing is more important for him to remember than that basic business tenet I recently saw expressed with barbed pungency in a *Harvard Business Review* article. "Marketing opportunities?" the author of the article asked after taking certain types of manufacturers to task. "Just come up with something that (a) works and (b) has the features customers want." In my opinion, that priceless gem should be pasted into the hat of every businessman, be he beginner or 50-year veteran. It states the essence of what is good business, what makes a business—and a businessman —a success.

The man going into business for himself also needs sufficient capital, but this is the least important factor. Just as a bad workman invariably complains that he has bad tools, so the bad businessman always wails that he does not have enough capital. It is entirely possible, even in this day and age, and will remain so in the marvel-filled future, to start small and grow big. There are always individuals and legitimate lending institutions willing to provide capital for a promising business at reasonable rates of interest or in exchange for reasonable quantities of stock.

To the man who feels himself qualified to go into business for himself, I say, "Start now!" There is no time like the present to get in on the ground floor and take full advantage of the rising trend and of the new and unprecedented opportunities that present themselves in dozens of fields. Large fortunes will be made in the next two decades by men who are beginners today. The most exciting and promising golden age in the world's history lies before us.

Starting your business career now?

If you are, I repeat—even more enthusiastically —what I said in 1958: I envy your chances. I wish I could take them for you. It would be fun to do it all over again!

3.
TWO PATHS TO THE TOP

GUIDELINES TO HELP
THE BUDDING EXECUTIVE DECIDE
WHETHER HIS FUTURE LIES IN
BIG BUSINESS OR SMALL

Recently it was estimated that there were some 120,000 millionaires in the United States—105,000 *more* than there had been in 1948. This astounding 700-percent jump in the number of American millionaires in little more than 20 years forcefully underlines what I have already emphasized: There is more opportunity to achieve success in business today than at any previous time in history.

Countless business leaders agree, predict even bigger and better things yet to come and are banking immense amounts of capital on their predictions. The essence of all such prophecies has been boiled down into two simple, but striking, sentences by Tex Thornton. "There's really no place to stop," he has declared. "We will never reach our destination."

Thornton's statements can hardly be taken lightly. He is the head of Litton Industries, a titan of the business world that, according to published accounts, "made him a millionaire 40 times over . . . and made millionaires of 20 other Litton executives" in a single decade.

It should be obvious what these statistics and prognostications mean for the beginner in business. Today's college graduates and budding executives can embark on business careers confident—if a play on words is permitted—that in this space age, the sky is no longer the limit.

Not only does our present era offer unprecedented opportunity, but the tyro is given an infinite choice of immediate opportunities for starting and building his career. The worried college grad of yesteryear who, diploma in hand, wandered forth from the groves of academe to search desperately for a job—almost any job—is but a faded memory. Nowadays, corporate mountains come to seek matriculated Mohammeds long before graduation day. Management recruiters for the nation's executive-hungry companies are familiar figures on college campuses, and they scrutinize likely candidates as covetously as professional-football scouts eye star quarterbacks.

A promising young man can all but write his own ticket. A dozen or more firms will vie for his services, offering him starting salaries that may well go into the five-figure range. There is certainly no need for him to grab blindly; he need only accept the offer that attracts him most.

On the job, the novice may expect to receive every aid and assistance, not only in acclimating himself to his new environment but also in training and grooming himself for rapid promotion. If he demonstrates ability, he soon finds other companies and executive headhunters wooing him with promises of more pay and perquisites, greater responsibility and better prospects for even further promotion.

In over 50 years as an active businessman, I've never seen anything to equal the currently prevailing climate of opportunity. But there is little need for additional prefatory comment. I assume anyone reading this book is already aware of the range and number of employment opportunities available to young executives.

However, although the ointment is rich and practically fly-free, the tyro *is* confronted by one very important choice even before he gets up to the starting line: Is he a big- or a small-business type? It is this problem, which has received comparatively little general attention, that I intend to explore.

Where would the budding executive function best and most fully realize his potential—in the highly organized, structured work situations found in most giant corporations or in the less formal environment usually characteristic of smaller companies?

These questions are seldom asked and even less frequently probed and analyzed to the extent they deserve. Each year, very large numbers of men leave college and go automatically into big business.

"One reason why seniors prefer big business is that the big companies go after them and the small ones don't," William H. Whyte, Jr., has written.

Furthermore, it has been my experience that

both executive-job seekers and recruiters are often prone to ignore varying individual potential quotients vis-à-vis big versus small business.

True, there are many men who, because of their nature, intellectual and emotional patterning and a host of other factors, are best fitted to work for large corporations. They function more efficiently, advance more rapidly and are personally more content in structured work situations, interacting with others as part of a complex organization. They are content to be cogs until they can become progressively larger gears—and, hopefully, at last the generator—in the intricate machinery.

There are multitudes of fine big-business executives, and innumerable large and eminently successful companies would not consider employing managers of any different stripe. Like it or not, the combination of organization man and structured organization *does* often work very well. Some of the nation's most tightly compartmented corporations are among the ones that show the highest earnings and profits and continue to grow steadily.

An able executive suited to structured work situations has an excellent chance of achieving success in a large company. If nothing else, the depth and definition of the vertical lines on the organization chart guide his course, preventing him from straying into unmapped—and, for his nature and temperament, alien and hostile—terrain. Although I have no statistics, it is a certainty that a sizable number of America's millionaire businessmen reached the magical seven-figure bracket step by step, via the strictly structured path.

On the other hand, there is a diametrically opposed species of individual much more likely to succeed in a small-business environment. The Harvard Graduate School of Business Administration is one leading educational institution noted for recognizing and encouraging men of this type. Its Student Small Business Placement Program (S.S.B.P.P.) has done yeoman work separating the small- from the big-business types and helping the former find their way into work situations for which they, their personalities and potentials are best fitted. The underlying principle of the program is that many an executive whose qualities would make him an outstanding small-business manager is stultified and rendered impotent in a big-business atmosphere.

S.S.B.P.P. spokesmen argue there are three general categories of small-business executives: those who excel in small business per se; those whose forte is small management, in big business or small; and those who'd do best buying equity in a small firm and managing it themselves.

Professor Myles L. Mace of the Harvard Graduate School of Business Administration maintains that many business students abhor the thought of "becoming nothing more than serial numbers in a large organization." And, he says, "they have an abiding fear that they will not have a chance to demonstrate their abilities in an environment that will recognize their contributions. They don't think this can be done in a large company. . . . It is not entirely true, but . . . they think it is."

Frank L. Tucker, dean of the Faculty for External Affairs of the same institution, declares, "It is my firm belief that some people were born to be in small business. They have a certain kind of per-

sonality that wants a wide scope for its abilities
. . . a strong desire for freedom and independence
and, at least sometimes, a desire to make a lot of
money fast."

Obviously, not every aspiring executive can at-
tend the Harvard Graduate School of Business Administration and benefit from its Student Small
Business Placement Program. However, just about
any intelligent neophyte manager can go a considerable way toward determining for himself
whether he is best fitted for big business or small.

He may avail himself of the sophisticated aptitude and psychometric tests that can provide in-
sights into the size and kind of business operations
that would be most compatible for him and offer
the greatest degree of dovetailing corporate and
personal needs and motivations—and, hence, the
best milieu in which to grow. These personal audits,
voluntarily and privately taken, are a very far cry
from the automated and mechanized tests that
seem to reject men of independent spirit and, instead, favor specimens of that stock figure, the
organization-man drone.

In any case, the tyro should make a careful,
detailed—and, above all, honest—study and appraisal of himself. During the five decades of my
own business career, I have frequently observed
that all too many men know less about themselves
than they do about almost any subject under the
sun. And, whatever knowledge they *do* possess
about themselves, they are virtually inarticulate
when it comes to describing or discussing it. Long
ago I hit upon a variant of an old childhood game
to gain some insight into the personality of applicants for executive positions. Once an interview

with an individual began, I asked the following question:

"If you were required to describe yourself and your views and attitudes on business in three sentences and no more, what would those sentences be?"

The answers I have received have run an encyclopedic gamut, and space doesn't permit the digression that would be necessary to discuss them even in the sketchiest manner. However, they provided reliable indications of the individual's true personality and innermost thoughts, if for no other reason than that it is human under such circumstances to state first things first. And the replies generally showed whether the applicant was basically more inclined to thrive in structured or in less formal work situations.

An aspiring business executive's personal inventory should be complete. For, as one management consultant was quoted in *Nation's Business* as saying, "if you do not have a carefully detailed career plan, and most people don't, you will do well to analyze all phases of your situation as objectively and completely as possible."

And, I might add, the analysis should be examined in light of the two contrasting work situations offered by big business and small. Naturally, if the personal inventory is to have any value, the individual must be familiar with the key characteristics of each sector of business. I've already touched upon a few. It might be well to examine these and some others more closely.

Let's start with big business. Unquestionably, large companies offer more safety, security and shelter than small ones. All other things being equal, it stands to reason that a corporate behemoth with annual sales of a billion dollars is less likely to have worries about the future than a firm that grosses, say, a million dollars a year. The former is better fixed than the latter to roll with the punches of temporary setbacks or to ride out economic storms.

The security factor extends all the way down to the most junior executive. In many giant corporations, even a manager of mediocre ability may enjoy a considerable degree of job security. Being one among many, his faults and failings will not be too noticeable. In some huge companies, an executive who survives his first two years or so just about enjoys job tenure. He may not get very high on the ladder, but he can cling to some rung with relative ease. Then, many large firms offer virtually automatic pay raises, bonuses, profit sharing, long vacations, stock options, hospitalization plans, retirement plans and other benefits appealing to the security-minded. Admittedly, some of these aren't of paramount interest to truly enterprising men, but there are more positive attractions for them.

Bigness itself often exerts a strong draw. Some years ago, I was much impressed by the evident potentials of a young man who intended making a business career, and I offered him a job with one of my firms. "No, thanks." He shook his head. "Since I've made up my mind to climb, I want to tackle the biggest pyramid I can find."

He obtained a bottom-layer executive job with one of the nation's ten largest corporations and is now one of its vice-presidents. We've remained friends and, when he was in Europe recently, he stopped to see me in England. He told me he never regretted his original decision. "At each stage, I felt I'd accomplished more than if I'd reached the next higher level in a small organization," he said. "Maybe the competition hasn't been as stiff as it would have been in a small firm, but there was much more of it, and that's always made each success seem greater and more gratifying."

Most huge companies have widely scattered branches and subsidiaries. More than a few executives state that this aspect appeals strongly to them. It is understandable. There is excitement, even adventure, in being rushed out to take over the Tokyo office or to clean up the mess that has suddenly developed in the Caracas plant. Other advantages enjoyed by big-business managers are the facilities, expert advice and scientific and technological aids at their disposal. These are seldom equally available in small companies.

But big business has drawbacks, too. The executive must, to some degree, submerge his individuality in that of the organization; while he need not become a faceless number, he will not give many virtuoso performances, either. Cog, little gear, big gear or even generator, he remains *part* of a complex apparatus that, by its very nature, cannot always function with optimum speed and smoothness.

A familiar big-business handicap and source of executive frustration is that, even at best, the structured organization is still likely to be cumbersome. For example, in such a company it's seldom possible to find one man who can quickly give an answer or make a decision. "In a big outfit, it takes three days to round up the three committees that'll spend the next three weeks mulling the question at hand," a veteran entrepreneur grumbled to me not long ago. This, of course, is an exaggeration, but the behemoths *do* frequently get bogged down in procedural rules, committee meetings and other forms of folderol that cause able, imaginative managers to lose—or tear—their hair.

Organization also tends to proliferate administrative departments, paper work and red tape, reducing flexibility and eventually leading to hardening of the company arteries.

Small business offers the success-seeking executive an entirely different mix of advantages, disadvantages, problems and challenges. For instance, the small-business executive won't be a specialist for long, since the company's size will not permit honeycombed compartmentalization. He may spend a year in production, then shift to merchandising. Or, after he has acquired a little seasoning, he may well find himself wearing several hats at the same time.

I know this from the early days of my own career. After having gained a bare sufficiency of all-round experience, I became a small—a very small—businessman in the oil fields. As such, I was my own drilling superintendent, purchasing agent, salesman, bookkeeper and just about anything else one could imagine. Had they actually existed, my various hats would have filled my cubbyhole office from floor to ceiling and wall to wall.

The small-business manager seldom enjoys as much security as his big-business counterpart, but he usually has more independence. This is not pure blessing, for he consequently carries a greater load of personal responsibility, with attendant risks to his job and career. He will frequently need to make his own decisions and may often feel very much out on a sagging limb if he has made a serious mistake.

Withal, there is liable to be greater operational efficiency in a small firm than in a large one. In the former, it is usually possible to find that one man who can say yes or no on the spot. The individual in small business has a far greater chance to exercise his individuality and initiative and to innovate and improvise. The small company is seldom wagged by its administrative tail; a telephone call or a five-minute chat will often accomplish what would require endless memorandums and committee meetings in a giant-sized firm.

Parenthetically, it is interesting to note that some huge concerns concede all this and are seeking to find happy mediums. "Many [large corporations] are doing effective concrete things to stimulate the creative atmosphere of small business," says Harvard Graduate School's Professor Mace.

Often cited as examples are W. R. Grace and Company and Thiokol Chemical Corporation. The former has many divisions, subsidiaries and partly owned companies, each of which is said to enjoy a remarkable degree of autonomy. The latter is credited with wedding the best of the big and the small through a project-management method.

Let me emphatically state that I acknowledge the achievements of the nation's great, structured organizations and am aware of the many production and distribution miracles they have performed. However, I, personally, have always remained at heart a small businessman. My associates and I have consistently sought to maintain small-business flexibility, creativity and efficiency. As an example, one of the companies in which I hold a substantial interest employs an overall total of 450 people. A competing firm does about five times the gross business but has 400 paper-pushing employees in its administrative offices alone. The difference is that the executives of my company operate in a loosely organized, highly flexible manner. Believe it or not, the firm does not even have a formal organization chart. Each manager knows his job, does it and couldn't care less what title, if any, is painted on his office door.

But what works well for J. Paul Getty and his associates may not work at all for the next man. Each person must determine which type of business shoe fits him best and will carry him farthest. Unfortunately, there are no infallible gauges for the novice, but I do think that some reasonable, helpful departure points can be provided. An intelligent young man may check these against his personal inventory and begin to form some conclusions about which of the two paths—the big- or the small-business route—he wishes to follow.

1. As a rule, giant corporations tend to offer structured work situations. Employed by such firms, the young executive will have greater security than in small firms, but he must keep a rein on his individuality. He will, in most cases, be required to conform, to play the game according to the book. He must, at least in the beginning, accept the fact that he is more or less anonymous and should not be dismayed to find himself in the type of work situation Professor Mace has called "the civil service of big business."

2. Generally, structured organizations produce

49

specialist executives. Big companies offer ample opportunity for advancement, but prospects of gaining wide experience or a broad business perspective are not as good as in smaller companies.

3. The average manager in the average large corporation needs to restrain many of his impulses to make independent decisions or to take unilateral action. He is always restricted to some degree by company policy that may well be formulated in a home office located 2000 linear miles away and a million light-years away insofar as his immediate problems are concerned. Such restrictions are counterbalanced by the fact that if something goes wrong, the chances that his head will roll are greatly reduced.

4. The small company will usually allow the neophyte manager to show and exercise his individuality. The executive will be bound by fewer rules, and he will encounter many situations in which he will have to make his own rules as he goes along. But remember, the smaller the group, the more clearly visible is each individual in it and the easier it is to observe his actions, good, bad or indifferent.

5. In a small business, a manager is likely to learn quite a bit about what goes on in departments other than his own. His experience will be much broader than that of the specialist, but even this presents dangers. A man establishing an excellent record in, say, two different departments and then, for whatever reason, failing in a third may find his earlier achievements forgotten and learn that his one strike is enough to put him out.

6. In sum, the manager in a small business will have to do much of his own thinking, decision

making and implementing of those decisions. But, while he may get credit for his accomplishments, he will certainly have to take all the consequences for his blunders.

There are advantages and disadvantages to any work situation. Only the individual himself can make up his mind which sector—the big or the small—appeals to him most and promises him the best chance of proving himself and achieving his success.

Luckily, under the business conditions that prevail—and that I believe will continue to prevail throughout the foreseeable future—the beginner's initial decision does not imply a lifetime commitment. Nowadays, the executive who spends all or even a major portion of his career with the same company is a rare bird indeed. It is a universally accepted fact of business life that modern managers maintain a high degree of job mobility, particularly in the early stages of their careers. "Changing jobs is part of one's own selective process," declares Alan Wolfley, financial vice-president of Scovill Manufacturing Company.

Personnel-selection specialist Jack H. McQuaig went so far as to write, "It is perfectly normal for a man to try four or five different jobs in his first three or four years at work." Frankly, I think that's carrying the job-mobility concept a shade too far. I'd be inclined to view a manager who'd held five different jobs in three years with skepticism, if not downright suspicion. However, the young executive *will* move around during his first few years, and, as long as he does it within reason, no prospective employer will think the less of him for it.

Thus, if a budding executive adds up all the

credits of big and small business and he still cannot arrive at a clear-cut decision, he can certainly accept what appears to be the happier compromise in either sector. If, after having given both the job and himself a fair trial, he finds he'd rather work in a structured organization than in a small company, or vice versa, he can always shift.

After trying both the big and the small, he should have a clear picture of what he has to gain or to lose in each type of work situation and which fits his nature and personality better. The same holds true for the man who does make a definite initial decision and chooses, for instance, small business and then discovers that he's made a mistake. He, too, can always change.

Once the individual finally determines which of the twofold paths to success will allow him to travel the farthest and fastest, he is well on his way to the top. Provided he has what it takes to make the climb, he will reach his goals along either route.

The opportunities are all there, waiting for those—be they big- or small-business-oriented—who will make the most of them. America's rapidly multiplying millionaires prove that beyond the shadow of a doubt.

4.
FAMILIARITY CAN BREED CONTENT

IN TODAY'S CORPORATE COMPLEX, THE JACK-OF-ALL-TRADES HAS A GOOD CHANCE OF WINDING UP THE MASTER

Some years ago, a company in which I held a substantial interest was about to embark on an extensive plant-modernization and expansion program. A key portion of the program called for a very large investment in a particular type of production machinery.

Machinery manufacturers had been contacted. They had submitted information and specifications on all their available models. Appropriate company executives, engineers and technical experts had made the customary studies and comparisons and had determined which was the best among the models offered. Orders for the equipment finally selected were about to be placed.

Luckily for the company, one of its executives

—a young man I shall call Howard Tracy—took it upon himself to voice objection at the last moment. Somewhat timorously—for he was a very junior executive—Tracy went to his superiors and told them he'd learned of an obscure machine-manufacturing firm that had developed, and was even then testing, a vastly improved model, one that was many years ahead of all existing types.

Howard Tracy reasonably argued that if the equipment under test by the manufacturer proved out, it would make all comparable machinery—including that which the company was about to order—woefully obsolete and inadequate.

Tracy's superiors listened but were rather skeptical. They'd never heard of the manufacturer in question and found it difficult to believe the apparently extravagant claims being made for the machinery. Nonetheless, they finally agreed to postpone ordering new equipment until they made the necessary inquiries and investigations of the machine-manufacturing firm.

In the end, the new model did indeed live up to all the claims that had been made for it and proved far superior to anything of its kind on the market. Naturally, company plans were immediately revised. The radically improved model, rather than the type previously contemplated for purchase, was ordered, eventually received and placed into highly profitable operation.

Thanks to Howard Tracy's last-minute entry onto the scene, the company was prevented from making a large capital outlay for machinery that would have been soon rendered obsolete. Instead, the company obtained the very latest and finest equipment well ahead of its competitors and was able to greatly increase output even while lowering production costs and, consequently, prices.

Now, as good an example as this is of an individual executive's alertness and enterprise, it is not yet the full story. You see, Howard Tracy was not a technical expert or an engineer. He was not even a production-side executive. Odd as it may sound, he was actually employed in the company's marketing division. His duties were concerned with sales, not with production.

When the incidents I've just described were brought to my attention, I determined to find out more about Howard Tracy. I learned that he did his own work extremely well, even brilliantly. He had a fine record with the company and was already marked as a "comer." I made arrangements to have lunch with him one day.

"You've probably saved the company quite a bit of money, and you've certainly been instrumental in placing it in an excellent position productionwise," I told him when we met. Then I asked, "But how is it that you know so much about machinery?"

"I actually know very little about it," the young man confessed amiably. "You see, I was present at several meetings where the plant-modernization program was discussed. I figured it would be a good idea to familiarize myself with the production end and did some reading up on the subject. That's how I ran across the item about the new machinery."

In the course of his "reading up," Tracy had come across a small machine manufacturers' trade journal that had a very limited circulation. It was from a story in this publication that he first learned about the newly developed equipment. Realizing its potentials and implications, he'd done some additional research on his own time and had then gone to his superiors with the information he had gathered.

Further conversation with young Tracy demonstrated that he had a keen interest in the company and just about everything that could affect it, its operations or its future. He was not just another marketing-department executive. He obviously had a remarkably clear understanding of all phases of the company's activities and was eager to increase his knowledge wherever possible.

I recognized that this was no narrowly limited specialist with a straitjacketed imagination. He was not burdened with any built-in blinders that prevented him from seeing anything but the comparatively restricted horizons of his own particular job and department.

Before our luncheon meeting was over, I knew that Howard Tracy was an exceptional young executive and felt that he was very probably headed for the top. My judgment was fully borne out in the next few years, during which time Tracy moved with remarkable rapidity into the uppermost echelons of corporate management. Since 1962—before he had reached his 31st birthday—he has been the head of a large and steadily growing company.

Granted that Howard Tracy had all the basic equipment to make him an intelligent and able executive. However, I'm inclined to believe that his spectacular rise can be attributed in no small degree to his drive to acquaint himself with all aspects of the business in which he chose to make his career. His desire to be familiar with the requirements, operations and problems of departments other than his own, of the company and the industry as a whole, did much to help boost him to the top of the heap.

There is an old adage that holds that "familiarity breeds contempt." I'll agree that this is true in some instances and under certain conditions—when the word *familiarity* is used to connote *undue* intimacy.

But the word has other meanings as well. It is also defined as meaning a close or full acquaintance with something. When used in this sense, it can be postulated that familiarity is quite likely to breed content rather than contempt.

Nowhere is this more evident or valid than in business and among businessmen.

All else being equal, the company whose executives are most familiar with the multitudinous facets of its operation is the company most likely to survive and thrive, even in the face of the heaviest competition and under the most trying economic conditions.

Again assuming other considerations to be equal, the executive who most thoroughly familiarizes himself with the diverse factors that could involve or affect the company for which he works is the executive most likely to achieve success in his business career.

The ideal businessman, the one with the 100-percent-plus assurance of attaining success, would, of course, be the man who is completely familiar with everything that has even the remotest conceivable connection with or influence on his business. Needless to say, there can be no such ideal businessman, for the complexity of modern business precludes any mortal from grasping and following every detail of the constantly changing present-day business picture.

Nevertheless, the man who hopes to rise above the lower-middle echelons of business management must be familiar with countless facets of his company's operation, the field or industry in which it is engaged and general economic trends and conditions.

It is by no means enough for the executive to know his own job thoroughly. If that is all he knows, the job he holds is the only one for which he is at all suited. And even then, unless the position is one that requires no imagination or enterprise, he will not be able to perform the job well. A man with narrowly limited perspectives cannot move beyond those limits, and the course of his career is charted for him——to a dead end.

What, then, are the matters with which an able and ambitious executive should familiarize himself?

Precise answers to this question are difficult to provide, for they would necessarily differ greatly from one instance to the next. Nonetheless, there are certain basics, certain areas with which every executive should be familiar if he aspires to reach the top brackets.

I have listed some of these basics below. While their relative importance will vary with each individual case, they are all valid and, to a greater or lesser extent, all universally applicable.

1. *One's own self.* The business executive must be able to appraise his own capabilities and limitations honestly. He should form the habit of periodically making an objective inventory of him-

self, doing it, if necessary, literally, using pencil and paper. The debits and credits should be noted and taken into account. Traits, qualities and characteristics on the plus side should be exploited to the full, while every effort should be made to correct those that appear on the minus side of the real or imaginary ledger.

One extremely successful businessman I know tells me that he has been rating himself every six months for the past 20 years. His method is simple: He uses a standard personnel-evaluation sheet and grades himself in the same manner as he would a subordinate employee. He claims this private system of self-evaluation has enabled him to recognize and capitalize on his strong points and to identify and thus try to correct his deficiencies. He declares the system has worked wonders and has contributed in no small degree to his success.

Whether or not an executive actually writes his personal inventory down on paper isn't important. It is important only that he know himself well enough to be able to plan a logical and attainable program for his own development. The plan may be flexible; it can be revised as the individual re-evaluates his potential in the light of additional knowledge or experience he has gained. But he must have a plan that charts his course. If he does not have one, if the executive is not totally familiar with his own strengths and weaknesses, his capabilities and shortcomings, he is very likely to flounder aimlessly and his career will be mediocre, because it has no direction or ordered, rational basis.

2. *Job.* It hardly need be said that an execu-

tive must know his own job thoroughly. But it is not sufficient for him to know his own duties and responsibilities. He must be familiar with their significance in relation to the company's overall policies and operations. Furthermore, there should be nothing passive about his familiarity with his job. He must never be satisfied with things as they are but must be constantly alert and seeking ways by which he can do his work more efficiently.

3. *Department or section.* What holds for the executive's own job also holds for the section or department in which he is employed. He must be familiar with the operations of his department and understand clearly how they function within the company and in relation to other departments and to suppliers and customers.

4. *The company.* It is difficult—and not infrequently impossible—to make an integral part of a complicated machine function properly unless one is familiar with the workings of the entire machine. I doubt seriously if an automobile mechanic could do a very good job of tuning a carburetor unless he was acquainted with the principles of the internal-combustion engine.

And so it is with the business executive. The business firm, the company, is a complex functioning apparatus made up of many interdependent and interacting parts. In order to perform his duties properly, the executive must be completely familiar with the company as a whole—with its history, organization, policies and operations. The more he knows about these things, the better he will be equipped to accept increased responsibility and to direct larger segments of the whole—and, eventually, the whole itself.

5. *Personnel.* In a sense, every executive is a personnel manager. He must deal constantly with personnel on three separate levels—his subordinates, individuals who are his equals on the organization chart and, finally, his superiors.

The good executive makes it his business to be conversant with the responsibilities and problems of those under him. He will even take a personal interest in the welfare of his subordinates. Nothing builds employee morale faster than a boss who remembers that the janitor's wife had a baby a week ago and takes the trouble to ask the proud father how mother and child are coming along. Such things may seem small on the surface, but they can achieve more results in improving morale and increasing efficiency than the most elaborate and costly employee-relations programs.

The executive must be acquainted with his equals. He must know them and get along with them. He should be familiar with their attitudes and outlooks, their personalities and peculiarities, in order that his relations with them may be as free of friction or misunderstanding as possible. There will, naturally, be some disagreement among equals, but familiarity in the sense of close acquaintance and understanding will make for generally cooperative relationships.

An executive must also know his superiors, in order to facilitate their work and his. There should be no bootlicking, but things move much more smoothly if an executive is familiar with the personalities and characteristics, the customs and policies, the likes and dislikes of his superiors.

For instance, one boss might prefer to have plans or problems presented to him in a terse, skeletonized outline, while another might insist on being given all the details the first time around. Or, as a more extreme example, the boss may be a little hard-of-hearing and, people being what they are, might well be reluctant to admit it. Knowing this, a subordinate can pretend to be ignorant of this and simply speak a little louder in his presence. Such things do not constitute bootlicking; they are simple human courtesies.

Dealing with people, with personnel—be they subordinates, equals or superiors—is not always easy. Sometimes it can be exceedingly difficult. The ability to deal with them, to know and understand them, is one of the key qualities that separate the man-sized executive timber from the boy-sized chips who will never make the grade into the upper echelons of management.

6. *Industry or field.* The higher a man sets his sights, the more he must know and understand about the field or industry in which he and his company are engaged. An executive in the XYZ Doorknob Company is well advised to remain abreast of all developments in the doorknob industry. He should know as much as possible about what competing firms are doing and familiarize himself with what's going on among the company's suppliers and customers. Only thus can he be alert to opportunities that present themselves and be forewarned about problems that might develop.

7. *Overall business and economic trends and conditions.* Today, the successful businessman must be something of a business analyst and economist. Few, indeed, are the companies that are completely independent of or impervious to the influences of general trends and conditions. A

forthcoming strike in the steel industry can have ramifications that seriously influence the operations of a diaper manufacturer. An economic crisis in Ruritania could conceivably cause repercussions that would affect the raw-material supplies—or even the sales—of a toy manufacturer in Hackensack. A sudden change in U.S. Government policy or a partisan tussle in Congress can—and often does—set off a chain reaction that leaves its mark on the profit-and-loss statements of a thousand and one business firms across the nation.

Any executive who seriously wants to reach the top must broaden his range of interests and familiarize himself with business and economic matters far beyond the realm of his own immediate field. He cannot begin to do this too soon. Even the most junior of executives can find no better way to invest his spare time than by boning up on general business and economic subjects and by closely following all current developments.

The successful businessman is the one who can, in an appreciable percentage of instances, correctly foresee developments, promptly take advantage of emerging opportunities and effectively forestall problems. No businessman can have a perfect batting average, but it is the man with the highest prediction-and-prevention record who reaches the top most quickly and remains there most securely.

These are some of the more important things with which an executive should be familiar if he wants to achieve success in the business world. I certainly do not suggest that it is easy to gain the necessary knowledge and attain the necessary degree of familiarity with the matters I have listed. Quite to the contrary, I would be the first to warn that much hard work is needed—hard and extra work that often has to be done on the individual's own time and at the expense of other, more pleasurable pursuits.

However, I maintain that the game is well worth the candle that may have to be burned far into the night. The rewards more than justify the effort.

The able and ambitious executive who is familiar with the varied aspects of business will advance rapidly. His familiarity will breed the kind of content that comes with the attainment of one's goals. Nothing succeeds like success, and there is no content like that which a man feels when he has achieved it.

5.
THE
EDUCATED
EXECUTIVE

**DESPITE TODAY'S EMPHASIS
ON SPECIALIZATION,
IT IS TRUER THAN EVER THAT
THE LADDER TO THE UPPER ECHELONS
IS BASED ON THE LIBERAL ARTS**

According to time-honored (if not entirely reliable) Horatio Alger tradition, almost any ambitious young man, with a lot of good fortune, could quickly reach the top of the ladder in the business world. The principal ingredient in the formula for success was luck: a careening carriage being pulled wildly along a street by a team of runaway horses—and, of course, inside the carriage, the terrified, nubile daughter of a multimillionaire. The young man needed only to fling himself on the horses' harness and, by dint of courage and brawn, bring beasts, carriage and the terrified, nubile daughter to a safe halt just short of disaster.

"My hero! You have saved my life!" the lovely damsel would breathe in gratitude. "I shall see that my father rewards you!"

Soon afterward, our hero would find himself happily and wealthily ensconced as—at the very least—a vice-president in one of the tycoon's giant companies and married, equally happily, to the tycoon's daughter.

I have no way of knowing how many, if any, Horatio Alger–style success stories were actually recorded in the history of American business. Certainly, the aspiring executive of today would have an extremely hard time trying to make his mark by waiting for a runaway Cadillac to pass him on Madison Avenue, Wacker Drive or Wilshire Boulevard. These days, reaching the upper rungs of the ladder of corporate success is hardly a matter of luck. Few, if any, of our modern-era business executives are born. Virtually all of them are made, in the sense that they are produced by various processes of education, training and experience.

Fortune magazine, which has established an enviable reputation among businessmen for its intensive coverage of the business world, has, at various times, sought to determine the qualities that make the nation's executives. I recall one survey conducted by the magazine that was aimed at gauging the level of education among executive personnel. In the course of the study, questionnaires were submitted to the chairmen, presidents, vice-presidents and other top-level executives of more than 800 U.S. companies. Results indicated that, of the 1700 upper-bracket management men responding, two out of every three were college graduates and one-fourth of the remainder had at least some undergraduate training.

Impressive as these statistics might seem—and

they do reflect a very high proportion of college graduates in the ranks of top management—a similar study made more recently, but among a smaller group of business leaders, showed that the proportion of college graduates was even higher: around 85 percent in this particular sampling. The educational qualifications of U.S. business executives are even more striking when some additional facts are considered. As *Fortune* pointed out, fewer than two percent of all American male college graduates have made Phi Beta Kappa. But in the upper strata of U.S. business management, the ratio of ΦBKs is five times greater than this: Nearly ten percent of the men holding top-level executive positions are entitled to sport ΦBK keys on their watch chains. And among the men who are at or near the apex of the business pyramid, some five percent made the dean's list, graduated *cum laude* or better or were chosen as valedictorians during their college careers. Eleven percent of these top executives were members of academic societies while attending college.

Charting the educational-attainment levels of younger executives through the years from 1900 to the present day, one is struck by the steady and unwavering upward curve. The conclusions are inescapable. The modern-day business executive obtains more formal education than his predecessors, and the better-educated executive is most likely to rise fastest and farthest.

Thus, on the face of things, it would appear that the nation's colleges and universities provide the best of all executive breeding grounds. It would appear that the principal prerequisite for success in business is a college education and that, once he has his sheepskin in hand, the college grad can scramble nimbly to the top of any corporate pyramid.

Unfortunately, first appearances are sometimes deceiving, and even the most accurate and carefully compiled statistics do not always reveal all the facets of the story they strive to tell. For many years, I—and seasoned businessmen of my acquaintance—have noted a very definite and increasing trend toward an overspecialization in education. In too many instances, the emphasis has been on the *technical* training of young men and women who intend to make their careers in the business world.

Admittedly, this is an age of specialization— a fact that holds as true for the business world as it does for, say, the medical profession. I'll be the first to grant that there is a great need for specialization in business, and I will even concede that business could not operate today without such specialists.

However, I regard as disheartening the growing trend toward overspecialization, toward one-track orientation among young executives, especially in their education. It seems that many young men are devoting an inordinately large portion of their academic lives to the study of the "useful disciplines," while ignoring those subjects that aid an individual in developing into a multidimensional human being.

Figures show that for a long time there has been a steady relative decline in the number of male college students who enroll in liberal-arts courses or who choose elective courses designed to broaden their cultural interests. "To the young executive, speculative thought is as foreign as the game of *boccie*," Walter Guzzardi, Jr., wrote in a magazine article. Culturally, Guzzardi concluded, the young American executive is a narrow man.

I think that at least some of the blame for this lies with our colleges and universities. I'm sure that a part of the current student unrest stems from feelings that the educational establishment is not in tune with the times. I can feel considerable sympathy for the intelligent college student who resents depersonalization. The universities have been selling the study of the useful disciplines and have, in a great many instances, done little to make the humanities appealing to young men who are eager to hear—and heed—guidance from school authorities or faculty members. Overemphasis on the useful disciplines is not so very far removed from the attitude that education should teach simple motor tasks. This attitude can produce a breed of depersonalized automatons. But the entering freshman student, desiring to prepare himself for a business career, is attracted by useful or practical courses; they seem to have intrinsic value. He is far less enthusiastic about the "soft" courses—dealing with the arts or the social sciences, for example—because he is not taught that they have any practical use.

It has been more than half a century since I attended college. Nonetheless, I can recall being less than satisfied by the teaching processes that prevailed—as it happened—at the University of California at Berkeley. I left Berkeley to complete my education at Oxford. There I found that the student was granted much greater freedom. Compared with Berkeley, there was infinitely more emphasis on the humanities. The student at Oxford was allowed to learn at his own pace and encouraged to read widely, far beyond the limits of any specialty or major.

Part of the blame for overspecialization can also be laid at the doorstep of some companies that, according to reliable accounts, prefer to hire the one-track type and shun the man with broader interests. Scores of books purport to provide infallible guides for executive selection. At least as many firms specialize in testing applicants for executive positions. Most of the books and testers say—or at least hint unmistakably—that an applicant's desirability falls in proportion to his cultural interests. On at least one test, according to Martin Gross, author of *The Brain Watchers*, evidence of a desire to visit fine-arts museums is taken as a warning that the candidate may not be 100 percent masculine.

Obviously, I disagree vigorously with such attitudes. While I am gratified that today's young executive is extremely well educated professionally and that he has the knowledge necessary to do his job well, I deplore the narrowness of his formal education and of his interests. I cannot help but feel that an education that fails to broaden one's outlook is an inadequate education. Neglect of the humanities—which give a student cultural interests and at least some understanding of people, the world and its institutions—can have no beneficial effect.

Today's top executive must be acutely aware of *all* that goes on around him. He must realize that his business—and business in general—is but a part of a social whole. He must understand that whole and all its parts. The head of a large corporation cannot seal himself within his corporation and shut out the rest of the world. There is far too much interdependence and interaction between business and other segments of society for that to be possible.

Beyond this, the one-track executive who has no grasp of matters outside the boundaries of his own narrow professionalism cannot do a proper job at the top levels of management, because he loses touch with human realities. Guzzardi has pointed out that the average young executive does not have much of the "stockholder mentality." "That white-haired old lady in sneakers in whose stout defense members of top management speak so vehemently and so often is a comparative stranger to the young executives," he charged. "They leave her fate to the boss."

To me, a veteran of more than half a century as a businessman, such attitudes on the part of young executives are intolerable. This new breed of executives seems to have lost, or quite possibly never had, the human understanding that makes all the difference in business. That this is at least in part due to their superspecialized education, their concentration on the useful disciplines and the consequent narrowing of their outlook is a reasonable assumption. It is evident that their useful disciplines haven't been useful enough to inculcate in them the simple truth, known to all successful businessmen, that although the stockholder may be a "white-haired old lady in sneakers," she is still a stockholder. Whether the young executive likes it or not, stockholders are human beings who have invested in the company that employs him and pays his salary. The stockholders, after all, *own* the company.

The statement that young executives leave the stockholder's fate to the boss is startling—and frightening. The man at the top of the corporate heap worries a great deal about the company's stockholders. He has always worried about them, for he was trained, whether through his formal education or through his early experience, that business has its responsibilities—to employees, to stockholders and to society. The fact that he worries about a stockholder's fate is, very probably, one of the principal reasons the boss is at the top while the young executives who do not have the "stockholder mentality" are still well down the ladder.

I know from personal experience that my own college education—especially at Oxford—served me in excellent stead throughout my business career. I learned much, and I have often applied the knowledge I gained to good advantage. But my studies in the humanities—subjects that expanded my cultural horizons—were of the greatest value. It was from these studies that I gained understanding and insight into the structure and development, the functioning and the dynamics of our world and our society. At the same time, I developed interests that have provided me with great pleasure and gratification throughout my life. They helped me be a better man—and a better businessman. My exposure to a wide variety of liberal-arts subjects made my mind more flexible, more receptive to new ideas, more readily aware of changing circumstances and, at the same time, more convinced of what constitutes real and

75

lasting values. In short, I do not hesitate to state flatly that I consider my liberal-arts education to have had far greater overall importance than any of the purely technical or professional subjects I studied.

I do not doubt that what I have said will appear to border on heresy for those who still cling to the concept of the business executive as a superspecialist. I am well aware that there are many companies that want their accountants to be accountants, their production experts to be production experts, and so on, and damn Aristotle and Zwingli.

Now, none of this is intended as a slap at business departments or management faculties in our universities and colleges. Both are excellent, generally conceded to be the best in the world. My point is that there has been a growing tendency toward specialization at the expense of broader subjects that not only expand the horizons of the students' minds but make them better human beings and, in the long run, better managers.

I particularly like what John Ciardi has written in his essay *An Ulcer, Gentlemen, Is an Unwritten Poem*. Ciardi argues, "Let [a man] spend too much of his life at the mechanics of practicality and either he must become something less than a man or his very mechanical efficiency will become impaired by the frustrations stored up in his irrational human personality. An ulcer . . . is an unkissed imagination taking its revenge for having been jilted."

Happily, there appears growing evidence that the trend toward producing superspecialized executives is being slowed or even reversed. There are indications that some of the nation's business leaders are recognizing the need for more diversified education of executive personnel. Take, for example, the survey conducted not long ago by Floyd A. Bond, Dick A. Leabo and Alfred W. Swinyard of the Graduate School of Business Administration of the University of Michigan. Sixty-six big-business chief executives were asked to give their opinions regarding the educational requirements they considered essential for top-level executives. Nearly one-third of the respondents said they believed an education in the liberal arts or humanities provided the best background, and this third did not suggest that *any* secondary field of emphasis was needed. Almost as many of the chief-executive officers interviewed believed that basic liberal-arts courses modified by secondary reference to business gave the tyro executive the best grounding. The third largest group held that liberal-arts training modified by a secondary emphasis on science and/or engineering would provide the business executive with the best and most helpful educational background.

As if this were not sufficient to indicate the shift in the business-education wind, witness the findings of two recent major studies that were conducted by the Ford Foundation and the Carnegie Corporation. The results of the two studies were published jointly and, although there were some areas of disagreement, one conclusion stood out sharply: Both studies strongly recommended that business education should be based solidly on the liberal arts.

I have discussed the problem of the narrowness of the young executive's education with more than a few business leaders with whom I am acquainted. Almost without exception, they—and this includes those holdovers of a past era who themselves received little or no formal education beyond grade school—agree that the executive whose mind has been trained for one-track business orientation is only half an executive.

The men who actually head the nation's largest corporations appreciate the importance of the humanities in the education of young men who hope to achieve success in business. Several major companies have even sponsored programs under which their more promising young executives could expand their cultural horizons by taking liberal-arts courses on company time and at company expense.

One of the first of these programs was launched by the Bell Telephone Company in 1953, when a group of the firm's executives attended a two-semester course at the Institute of Humanistic Studies at the University of Pennsylvania. Other companies have since followed suit, and many colleges and universities have developed special liberal-arts courses for executives. In addition, some corporations have gone in for crash programs, sending selected executives—not infrequently men who are already on the upper rungs of the corporate ladder—to seminars and courses designed to increase their knowledge and appreciation of matters cultural.

These companies understand that, although he may have a string of degrees after his name, the executive whose education has been almost entirely professional is not well equipped to understand the broader social implications of business.

He is most likely a rather empty man whose sole concern in life, to the point of obsession, is his job and the struggle for advancement. Success becomes the end in itself. It might surprise him to learn that his one-track preoccupation lessens his chances for success.

I assure you that if I were contemplating the establishment of, say, a new company or a foreign subsidiary, I would not rely on an executive with single-function orientation to conduct the negotiations. Not on your life—or, rather, not on my hopes and expectations of success.

The men I would choose for the task would have to solve problems and make decisions on the spot. Although they might conceivably be weak in certain technical areas, they would be well-rounded individuals whose education had enriched their intellect and judgment, rather than merely providing them with a degree of practical or technical know-how. Such has always been my policy, and I am firmly convinced that it is largely responsible for whatever successes I have achieved during the course of my business career.

Today's young executive has two choices: He can choose to be educated as a narrow specialist, little more than a technician, concentrating entirely on the useful disciplines and disdaining all else, or he can choose to become a well-rounded man—a man of taste, discernment, understanding and intellectual versatility. If he selects the former course of action, he is quite likely to remain a junior or middle-grade executive throughout his career. If he chooses the latter, he will greatly increase his chances of reaching the top, and he will enjoy life and himself much more in the process.

6.
HOW TO PICK THE RIGHT MAN

**SAGE ADVICE FOR
THE EXECUTIVE WHO WOULD
HIRE AND PROMOTE WISELY**

The problem of how to select the right men to fill executive jobs has been occupying, and in some instances preoccupying, many individuals in the business world for quite some time. Fully aware that no company can be any better than the people who run it, businessmen are ever hopeful of building management staffs made up of men who are paragons of all known or suspected virtues. Theoretically, there should be an ideal man for every position, but, in practice, this is seldom, if ever, the case. No one is without flaw. The perfect man—or, if you prefer, the complete executive—may be born someday in the distant future, but I am inclined to doubt that he will make his appearance in my lifetime or in that of anyone who reads this book. Hence, the selection of executive personnel boils down, as do just about all things in life, to accepting the fact that although perfection may be a goal, it is seldom attainable. Instead, one must find the most promising compromise, seeking out the man who seems best qualified for any given opening and who is thus the right man for that job.

Business management is largely a matter of decision, and there are few decisions more critical than those involved in hiring or promoting executive personnel, for the men ultimately picked will themselves be required to make decisions that can quite literally make or break the company that employs them. In recent years, the devising of yardsticks by which an individual's qualifications and potential may be measured has become at once a parlor game, an honored profession, an obsession and an industry in itself. Businessmen, personnel specialists, management consultants, psychologists and countless others have devoted vast energies to formulating lists of characteristics that, they claim, a man should possess if he is to be a successful executive. There is some agreement on certain fundamental and rather obvious qualities (for example, most sources concede that an executive should be "intelligent"); beyond such basics, the crystal ball is clouded.

But, then, there has never been anything like full agreement on what makes a man better or worse than his fellows. More than 2000 years ago, Plato theorized that human-behavior patterns are controlled by three factors: appetite, emotion and thought, all of which should function in harmony. However, Plato warned, "even in good men there is a lawless wild beast . . . which peers out in sleep." Aristotle argued that when any human qualities are carried to extremes, they become vices and that "good" qualities are those that lie midway between bad extremes. For example, ambition is the desirable middle ground between the bad extremes of laziness and avarice. Socioeconomic theorist Charles Fourier spent years painstakingly cataloging what he maintained were the 810—no more, no less—types of human character, while William James divided people into two groups, the "tough-minded" and the "tender-minded." Sigmund Freud injected the id, the ego and the super-ego—and a host of theories regarding sexual motivation—into the question of personality appraisal. William McDougall, an avant-gardist in social psychology, neatly explained human behavior with seven motivating "instincts"—flight, fight, curiosity, disgust, parental behavior, self-assertion and self-abasement.

The list of theorists and theories could be extended almost indefinitely without showing any appreciably greater degree of agreement. Nowadays, personality-and-aptitude testing has become a major industry, said to gross well over $50 million per year. A University of Texas Bureau of Business Research survey of 825 U.S. companies showed that 56 percent of the firms were using personality and aptitude tests in personnel selection. *Fortune* magazine placed the national average even higher. A single testing organization is reported to have more than 11,000 industrial clients on its books. Another large testing firm runs more than 35,000 job applicants—mostly for executive or supervisory jobs—through its test sieves each year. Whole schools of thought and even elaborate mystiques have grown up around the question of personnel—especially executive personnel—selection. Some business firms, it is said, have even turned to phrenology, physiognomic analysis, handwriting analysis and astrology in their frantic search for a surefire means of picking the right men.

Still, with hundreds of theories, systems and tests, no one has discovered a foolproof and universally applicable method for matching men to jobs. Invariably, we return to the basic question: What are the qualifications that serve to make a man a successful executive? This is a question that has never been fully answered. For over a century, American business leaders have been outspoken in their opinions on the subject, though often their opinions don't agree.

"It is heart service that counts," declared Andrew Carnegie. "You must capture and keep the heart of the original and supremely able man before his brain can do its best." "Above all, you must have tenacity," was Daniel Guggenheim's view. "That is the greatest quality. Without it, no man can possibly succeed." Cyrus H. McCormick maintained that the successful executive must love his work and remain in sound physical condition. J. P. Morgan's partner, George W. Perkins, claimed that the successful businessman should look upon his work as play. IBM's Thomas Watson held that the main thing was to "aim high and think in big figures." Charles P. McCormick of the McCormick spice company stated that he considered "loyalty the greatest characteristic trait needed in an executive." Alfred Sloan of General Motors said that understanding how to work with people, along with personality, represented "75 percent of the necessary equipment." Sears, Roebuck's Charles Caldwell defined the qualifications for an administrative executive as "mental ability, sociability, administrative skill, stability, predictability, drive, a sense of personal competitiveness and breadth of interests."

The controversy over what, precisely, makes the right man continues to rage. A few years ago, *Steel* magazine listed the "27 traits most common to good executives." These included "a superior level of intelligence," "creative ability," the fact that he "must have no special pressing problems with his wife" and that he "must have no serious health problems."

Fortune has reported that there is some consensus that "six dimensions" distinguish the executive elite from the "least good managers." The six traits are:

1. Initiative, assumption of responsibility and leadership
2. Job knowledge and skill
3. Dependability, thoroughness and follow-through
4. Getting along with people
5. Stability under pressure
6. Fine personal qualities and work habits

On the other hand, *Nation's Business,* having surveyed "America's top business decision makers and thinkers," cites *five* "most needed" executive skills:

1. Ability to be flexible and adapt to accelerated change
2. Ability to be imaginative and to innovate
3. Proficiency in controlling and reducing all expenses

4. Ability to mobilize and motivate men

5. Skill in coordinating and correlating forces within and outside your company

All these points are well taken and valid to some extent in selecting management personnel. All the traits mentioned are valuable for an executive to possess, but their relative importance will vary from one situation to another. And, obviously, there cannot be very many men who possess all these qualities in abundance. But such guidelines are by no means the end of the trait-listing game.

A widely selling book on executive selection lists "Five Hidden Traits That Shape a Man's Career," plus "Ten Magic Keys to a Man's Character." Another book, written by a management consultant, offers a "57-point checklist" to determine a man's qualifications for an executive position. Yet another book gives a "simple, easy 101-point personality-inventory guide" that, the author claims, will "bring the margin for error in executive selection down to an irreducible minimum."

All in all, if I may be permitted a somewhat skeptical observation, an applicant for an executive position who underwent all the available tests and interviews would be well past the retirement age before he completed them. Executive-personnel selection is far from an exact science.

I do not mean to imply that I consider all forms of personality, psychological and aptitude tests worthless. Properly used, and held within reasonable limits, such tests may provide a certain amount of valuable information. How valuable depends on many factors. For example, I rather imagine that familiarity has a strong bearing on the results of any test; an individual who has taken the same test or very similar ones earlier will be likely to score much differently from the man who takes a test for the first time. Even if the tests can be helpful, I am dubious that the average assembly-line personality or aptitude evaluation invariably proves or disproves an individual's qualifications for a job. Tests should hardly be the sole criterion by which an applicant is judged. Surely, his previous record and other pertinent data could conceivably outweigh almost any test scores.

In light of present trends, my views may be anachronistic, but I believe that responsibility for selecting personnel should rest primarily with those holding authority over the department in which there is an opening. The men who will be an applicant's superiors should be the ones to determine whether or not he measures up. These men are not infallible, but neither are the psychologists, management consultants and testers. The seasoned and successful executive usually achieves a fairly high batting average in hiring and promoting; his knowledge of the company's problems and his experience in dealing with people enable him to choose the right man at least as well as an outsider. If anything, the executive will be more careful, for he realizes that the efficiency of his own department—and thus, to some extent, his own success—will depend on the performance of his subordinates.

I know that I have long made it a policy to observe how the men an executive hires and promotes prove out, for this offers a usually reliable insight into the quality of the executive himself. If he consistently hires good men and if he is able to recognize and reward the most deserving among his subordinates, this is an indication of his own sound judgment and ability. If, on the other hand, a manager has a record of picking losers, I'm inclined to doubt his qualifications for the job he holds.

The selection of executive personnel divides naturally into two separate categories, each with its own particular problems. The first involves choosing a man from outside the organization to fill a vacancy, and this includes the recruitment of young men, mainly college graduates, for executive-trainee or junior-executive positions. The second involves the selection of men already in the organization for promotion to higher positions.

Whom to hire, which man to pick from among a dozen or a hundred applicants is, like so many other business problems, very much a matter of using common sense, drawing upon accumulated experience and instincts. No matter what checklists are used, the final choice of the man to fill an executive vacancy is still a question that should be settled by management decision. I believe that each executive should, within the framework of company policy, evolve his own standards for the men he has to hire.

To depend blindly on tests or arbitrary criteria set by some outside "expert" is to shirk management duty and to risk overlooking valuable human material. Certainly, a conscientious manager should exercise great care against the possibility that a tester's personal bias might influence his interpretations. For example, one much-publicized management consultant insists that an executive should have "no less than two and no more than three" children. Others feel constrained to ferret out the most intimate details of an applicant's sex life. And there are some "experts" who turn positively purple if an applicant displays the slightest sign of eccentricity in his dress.

These seem debatable criteria. I have known entirely too many crack executives who had no children or half a dozen. I can't really see how the answer to the question "Do you ever go to sleep at night without saying good night to your wife?" —which, by the way, is considered a key question on one widely used personality-evaluation test— helps determine whether or not a fourth assistant vice-president can do his job properly. As for eccentricity of dress—well, it strikes me as extremely unlikely that long hair or a penchant for argyle socks can drag an otherwise competent executive into the sloughs of inefficiency. The oil business, for example, has always had its share of rugged individualists. I've known more than a few crack managers in the industry who went straight to the top, even though they were types as likely to show up in the board room wearing Levi's and coonskin caps as gray flannel suits and homburgs.

Of course, many of the standards involved in choosing a man to fill a job vacancy depend on the job itself, the character of the company and other variables. As an obvious example, one would hardly try to make a Middle Eastern oil manager out of an individual who had spent his entire career as a staff man in the candy industry. Once the person responsible for hiring has a complete and detailed knowledge of the position that is open, he knows what particular qualifications are needed. The hunt for the right man thus is narrowed to a search for the individual who most closely meets the given requirements.

In hiring young men without previous experience, usually those who have just graduated from college, there are certain standards upon which one is almost forced to rely, because there is no actual work record to indicate the applicant's capabilities. I agree that even an executive trainee should be intelligent; he should be able to grasp the ideas expressed by others and to formulate and express his own. A beginner's *character* is also important; it would be folly to try to make a junior executive out of a young man with a long record of car theft. On the other hand, I do not subscribe to the theory that an applicant should be refused consideration because of a minor teen-age transgression or two. I myself played hooky from school when I was a youngster, but, of course, in those days truancy was punished in the woodshed and not in the courts.

The tyro's scholastic record is also important, but, again, not decisive. A straight-A average does not guarantee that a young man will be a good executive, nor is it proof positive of his intelligence or ability. I have known many efficient, even brilliant executives who received only mediocre marks in school, and I have also known men with dazzling scholastic records who achieved only mediocre business success, because they were tenacious but uninspired plodders.

An example from my own experience may help emphasize the point. Some years ago, the president of a company in which I hold a controlling interest waxed highly enthusiastic about a new executive who had been hired largely on the strength of his dazzling scholastic record. The new man was a Phi Beta Kappa, the winner of scholarships and awards and the showpiece product of a graduate school of business. By chance, I happened to meet the man soon after he started to work for the company. Although I found him unimpressive—a bland, neither-here-nor-there type—I remembered his sparkling academic record and said nothing that would in any way hinder his progress. I didn't have to say anything. Less than a year later, I learned he had been allowed to resign. The reason? A fault not really his own and not really to be counted against him. He was simply too much the scholar, too much the academic theoretician. His brilliance and knowledge were not spiced with the necessary touch of the hardheaded and practical—prosaic virtues, perhaps, but essential for getting things done.

Alertness, imagination, enthusiasm, ambition, business acumen—these are among the characteristics that help make a beginner a desirable applicant. And I might hazard to say that they are characteristics that seasoned executives can recognize during the course of a personal interview at least as well as testers can spot them from questionnaires.

In recent years, some companies have conducted large-scale campus-recruitment programs that, if published statistics are correct, have largely defeated their own ends. The turnover rate of young men recruited during these campaigns is said to be inordinately high—up to 75 percent during the first five years in some companies. Also, according to a recent article in *Nation's Business*, many of the companies have apparently sugar-coated the pill to an incredible degree. Discussing the recruiters' brochures that are distributed to students, *Business Week* reported, "Practically no brochure even mentioned the subject of work or otherwise indicated that the students would have to contribute something."

The desire to work and work hard is one of the most important of all qualifications a beginner can possess. I believe that the young man who seeks a business career wants to work hard, and this can compensate for many other shortcomings. The companies I own or control do not conduct campus-recruiting programs. Young men who apply for jobs with my companies are impressed with the fact that they will be expected to work very hard indeed, and my companies have never suffered from any shortage of job applicants.

Certainly, anyone who is being considered for an executive or junior-executive position is entitled to have all the facts, the bad along with the good, laid on the line. He should be told frankly what problems he will be inheriting if he gets the job—and what other problems he is likely to encounter if he continues up the ladder. The man with the potential for success will accept even the worst news as a challenge to his own ability.

The fledgling executive's personality is also a factor in establishing his relative desirability, but, in my mind, to only a limited extent. I agree that executives should be able to get along with people, that they should work in harmony with subordinates, equals and superiors. But an executive is hired to do his job and to get others to do theirs, not to reap high honors in a corporate popularity contest. Mr. Personality Plus is all too likely to worry more about what people think about him than about what they must accomplish on company time.

Needless to say, there is always a large element of chance involved in hiring a young and previously untried man. He is picked almost entirely on the basis of promise. On the other hand, the tyro can be more readily trained than the man who has already been employed and who has, in many instances, learned how to do things in ways that may not necessarily be preferred by his new employers.

But in hiring men with previous experience, the prospective employer does have concrete evidence of an applicant's ability—his past performance. What a man has done in the past generally can be taken as a fair indicator of what he will do in the future. From the employer's standpoint, there are only two types of men with previous experience: those who are unemployed and those who are working for another company and wish to make a change. If the man is unemployed, it is a sound idea to find out why. Was he fired for inefficiency or did he quit because he felt he wasn't getting anywhere? If an efficient executive with a good record becomes the victim of a merger or a change in top management and suddenly finds himself jobless, it is entirely reasonable to assume that he will be an equally efficient executive in a new position for which he is otherwise qualified. A sales executive who doubled the sales of his company and then quit when he found himself locked in with no opportunity for further advancement is likely to remain an energetic executive who will continue to produce when he moves to another firm.

Questions also need to be answered if the applicant is still employed elsewhere. It is important to know why he wants to make the change or to learn, if possible, if he is actually being eased out. Usually, an employed executive seeks a new job because he wants to make more money or have more opportunity. These are understandable motives, on the face of things. But, again, the astute businessman will probe a little further. There is always the chance that a man who wants more money may have an auction-block mentality and that he will soon be seeking yet higher bidders for his services. If he wants more opportunity with another firm, it is wise to make sure that he hasn't bungled the opportunities that his current company offered.

Beyond the question of hiring is the problem of selecting men for promotion. Here, I prefer to use what I call the "weight lifter's approach." It is by no means a quick or an easy way to tackle the problem, but I feel it's well worth the time and effort necessary, and it certainly achieves the highest percentage of right decisions. Put yourself in the shoes of a weight-lifting coach. If he wants to find out how much a new man can lift, he does not ask the newcomer to heft a 300-pound barbell at the beginning. The man is allowed to warm up gradually. He starts with, say, a 100-pound barbell. If he handles that without too much trouble, the weight is increased, by 20- or 40-pound increments, until the 300-pound mark is reached.

Now, just suppose that the man in question was told to start out immediately by trying to lift all 300 pounds. Even though it might be within his capabilities to lift it eventually, the chances are he would not be able to do so without a preliminary warm-up. Thus, he would have failed, even though he could have succeeded if he'd received a fair opportunity to prove himself.

The same principle applies to the problem of readying men so that they will be fully qualified for promotion. All too often, this principle is ignored in business. In fact, one of the most common corporate errors is to promote a man who, although he possesses the basic equipment, has not had the necessary warm-up before being thrust into a higher position. It is manifestly unfair to the man, and risky for the company, to suddenly give an executive far more responsibility than he is accustomed to having. The commonsense way to give a man an even break and, at the same time, to minimize risks for the company is to gradually and progressively increase his authority. And what holds for the tyro at the bottom of the ladder holds for all management personnel at all levels. The men who have better equipment and show more ability should always be trained and ready to take over a job on the next level.

When it comes to picking the man who gets the promotion, tests seem even less relevant than they are in hiring. Whether or not a man should be advanced to a bigger job should, I think, be decided largely by how he has performed previously in the company. How his proficiency is to be judged is a matter for management to decide. Local conditions and variables must necessarily influence the nature of the criteria used. Still, there are certain basic guidelines. For example, Charles W. Foreman, vice-president of United Parcel Service, has provided one succinct and, in my opinion, universally applicable yardstick for measuring which men are best qualified for promotion. Foreman holds that the true test lies in how an individual has handled the three basic materials with which all executives must work: money, time and people.

The executive's attitude toward the company's money is all-important. He must be acutely profit-conscious, unequivocally dedicated to the principle that every task, if humanly possible, should be translated into a profit. The executive who is promotable is the man who views the company's money as something that he is obliged to administer wisely and well, to see it spent with maximum care to achieve maximum results. How he handles company money is all the more significant because, after all, the higher he goes, the more money he will control.

As I recounted earlier, I took over active management of the Spartan Aircraft Corporation during World War Two at the request of Secretary of the Navy Frank Knox. It was a time of considerable stress in all industries and good personnel were scarce. There was one executive in the company who, according to his immediate superiors, deserved promotion. I was about to approve a boost in both salary and responsibility for him when I happened to learn, purely by accident, that he made a habit of bringing his personal letters to the office and having his secretary run them through a company postage meter.

I immediately discarded all idea of promoting the man and, indeed, let him know diplomatically that his resignation would be most welcome, the sooner the better. I explained my reasons to his superiors who had plumped so hard for him. True, the total amount involved was small—ten dollars, perhaps fifteen dollars, over many months. But the amount isn't what counted. The money was not only a loss to the company but, since we were working on government war contracts, a loss to the taxpayer. And, of course, I mentioned—quietly and *en passant*—that the man's acts constituted petty larceny.

All of us had reason to be glad that we had gotten rid of this particular man. He went to another company, where he received several promotions during the next few years, and then, not long after V-J Day, someone brought a newspaper story to my attention. It was an account of how this penny-ante postage pilferer had been arrested and had pleaded guilty to charges of embezzling more than $200,000 from the company for which he was working.

In the business world, time is scarcely less important than money. The eminently promotable executive is always one who knows how to budget his time. He does not squander time any more than he squanders money, and he does not cheat the company of the time he should devote to his work. The man who is most likely to move up the ladder is seldom tardy on the job and he is not likely to be the type who habitually leaves early. The good executive is also aware that time is important in other ways—that deadlines must be met.

As for people—well, management has been defined as "the art of directing human activities." The manager's principal task is not so much to do things himself as to direct other people in performing their duties. An executive who is unable to direct people is unable to do his job. The better he is at handling people, the better he is as an executive.

However, it's advisable to slice the evaluation even finer, to take into consideration other factors, tangible and intangible. For instance, there is the quality that some prefer to call resiliency—the ability to accept setbacks and criticism manfully, without going into a brooding blue funk. The outstanding man will accept the setbacks, take the criticism and, learning his lessons from both, will energetically strive to do better the next time. Also, the promotable man will certainly be an executive who does not hesitate to accept responsibility for any of his actions. As far as I am concerned, nothing eliminates an individual from consideration for promotion faster than the knowledge that he is a buck passer. And the higher a man rises in the organizational lineup, the more essential it is for him to be an individual of absolute integrity. If he does not stand by his decisions, accept his responsibilities, where necessary admit his mistakes and otherwise prove his honesty, an executive cannot move up; he can, at best, only remain where he is or—even better, from the company's standpoint —move out.

The man destined to climb the ladder of success most nimbly will also value knowledge, all knowledge, not just that which pertains directly to his specialty. He wants to learn, and he does learn. The more he knows about more things, the better his equipment for meeting the requirements of higher posts. Maturity—of judgment and of action —is another key asset that should be taken into consideration when promotion time rolls around.

The mature executive can live without panicking in an atmosphere of stress; he is stable and capable of handling emergency situations and problems. A company hard put to decide whether Jim or Tom should fill the assistant vice-president's opening, because in all other things the two men are equal, can decide the issue quickly by comparing their maturity. Which of the two men reacted best under stress?

While I obviously do not believe there are any hard-and-fast rules for executive selection, I do have my own ideas of what basic qualities a good executive should possess. These are intelligence, initiative, interest, integrity, imagination, leadership ability, loyalty, energy and enthusiasm—plus, providing the man has a previous employment record, the knowledge and experience necessary to do the job.

Such a man will naturally want reasonable compensation—in salary, commissions, stock options or other emoluments—and he will want assurance that his earnings will be increased if he does his new job well. However, if he is really good executive material, money alone will not be enough to make him leap at the position. He will want to be shown that he can use his imagination, talents and initiative, that he will be given the chance to show what he can do and the opportunity to advance further.

Whether he's concerned with promoting or with hiring, the seasoned businessman or executive will weigh all the data available on an applicant, size up his man and then make his management decision. By so doing, the businessman is proving his own ability. Jonathan Ogden Armour, once chairman of the meat-packing firm, summed it up many years ago when he was asked what traits he thought contributed most to a man's success in business. "The most valuable ability of all is the ability to select the men of ability," Armour declared. And therein lies the key to successful executive-personnel selection. Good executives can recognize other good men, and from these they can pick the best man, the right man, for the job.

7.
QUITTING TIME

WHEN AND HOW THE EXECUTIVE SHOULD UNDO THE BUSINESS TIES THAT BIND

Walter Jones was 37, an executive at the middle-management level, employed by the Noname Company. He was a fine manager with an excellent performance record; his superiors considered him to be a man of great ability and promise and valued his services highly.

There was only one thing wrong: Jones had held the same position for three years and had outgrown it. He wanted—and was eminently qualified to hold—a bigger, more responsible and more challenging job. Unfortunately, the Noname Company's executive-personnel situation was such that Walter Jones was locked in. Higher posts were held by competent men, all of whom had a long way to go before reaching retirement age. To make matters worse, there was very little chance that the company would embark on any important expansion programs in the foreseeable future.

Walter talked the matter over with his superiors. They assured him he would be moved up as soon as possible, but admitted this might not happen for several years. They did, however, offer Jones a substantial salary increase if he would continue in his job until a suitable vacancy occurred.

What would *you* do under similar circumstances?

This is a good question to ask yourself—and to answer as honestly as you can. What you would do —or think you would do—is quite possibly an indication of your success potential as a business executive.

No doubt, many men would be content to stay, to wait it out, comfortable, even smug, in the knowledge that they had a virtual sinecure, a guaranteed future. This sense of security would loom as ample justification for remaining on the old job, continuing to do all the same things until, at last, time and attrition provided opportunity and reward.

Not so Walter Jones.

Aware that he'd begun to chafe because he was ready and eager for more responsibility, Walter sensed that the chafing would soon develop into intense chronic irritation. He felt the long wait might well dull the edges of his enthusiasm. He feared that, as he got deeper and deeper into an already familiar groove, he would "run down," become a progressively less and less efficient and effective executive.

It was for these reasons that Jones decided to quit, without rancor but not without regret. He'd enjoyed working for the Noname Company, made many friends in the organization and would have liked to stay. Nonetheless, he knew he could not afford to interrupt the progress of his career with a long dead period. Thus, he resigned, moved to another company and moved up a notch to precisely the sort of challenging job he sought.

An oversimplified, too obvious example? Perhaps, but no more so than countless thousands of similar situations that will arise every year in the business world. Innumerable executives find themselves boxed in, unable to progress due to conditions within their companies—conditions over which they have no control. Ambitious, able executives of Walter Jones's caliber react—and act—as he did. Lesser men are likely to hang on and hope or vacillate, unable to make up their minds.

"The comers are movers," declares Dr. Frank McCabe, director of executive personnel for International Telephone and Telegraph. "If they can't move on to more responsible positions inside [a company], they'll go to another company."

William P. Lear, the aircraft-instruments entrepreneur who built Lear, Inc. (later Lear Siegler, Inc.), is even more outspoken, offering executives the following straight-from-the-shoulder advice:

"As soon as you've learned how to do your job as well as it can be done, ask for more responsibility in your company—or for a different job. If you don't get it, get the hell out!"

Such counsel would appear subversive, aimed at destroying all the oft-cited principles of executive loyalty to the company. But loyalty is a two-way street. As Dr. McCabe has noted, the loyalty of executives "depends upon the company's willingness to provide challenges and rewards in the job situation."

Stated simply, it all goes back to the old adage that you can't keep a good man down—or, rather, in the present context, that a good executive will not permit himself to be held back in his career. The best men, those with the greatest ability and drive, will refuse to stagnate anywhere along the line. They will get ahead, even if they have to go somewhere else.

To hold such men, to keep them within an organization, it is incumbent upon the organization to make sure it has the incentives upon which these men thrive. If a company cannot or will not provide these incentives, it has absolutely no grounds for complaint when its best men walk out.

Few, if any, of an executive's decisions are more important to him personally than those concerning the question of whether or not—and when and how—to quit a job he holds. Things being what they are in business and industry, these are decisions the average manager will have to make several times during the course of his career.

Estimates of executive turnover vary, but all tend to be on the high side. In his book *How to Pick Men*, Jack H. McQuaig maintains that it is "perfectly normal for a man to try four or five different jobs in his first three or four years at work." Some years ago, a survey conducted by McGraw-Hill indicated that one in every three key men in industry changes his job each year.

Chester Burger, author of *Survival in the Executive Jungle*, comments that "the average survival time in the executive jungle is short. Rare is the executive who has spent most of his working career with a single company."

Burger cites the results of one study of a group of middle-management executives that showed that 41 percent "survived in their last jobs for less than three years." And, he continues, still drawing on data obtained by the study, "three out of every four [middle-management men] switched jobs before they reached the ten-year gold-watch mark."

Obviously, not all of these men leave their jobs of their own accord. Some are "allowed to resign" under pressure. Others are squeezed out in mergers or consolidations. Still others are simply fired. Even among those who apparently leave of their own volition, there are many who quit because they have recognized the not always subtle signs that indicate the ax is about to fall. We are not interested here in any of these types of job leavers. Our concern is with the men who quit at their own option while they are in good standing with their companies.

Why do executives decide to quit under these circumstances? There are many answers. Recently, a well-known management-consultant firm conducted a survey, questioning 422 job-hunting executives in an effort to determine what motivated them to seek a change.

Foremost of the reasons was the desire for more responsibility and challenge, for a bigger job— plums not available in the companies for which the individuals concerned were currently working or by which they had been last employed. Next in importance was the desire for greater future opportunity. These, of course, are the same motivations that impelled Walter Jones to leave the Noname Company and seek greener pastures elsewhere, the chief motivations that, as Dr. Frank McCabe put it, cause the "comers" to be "movers."

More money—a larger immediate income—was the third most frequently cited reason for changing jobs. Now, I can readily understand any executive's desire to earn as high an income as possible. After all, he is performing a commercial service and is entitled to demand the maximum monetary reward he can obtain for that service.

On the other hand, it is frequently unwise to measure either jobs or men solely by a dollars-and-cents yardstick. Companies should always bear in mind the basic truth that a man who is interested only in money cannot be "bought" for very long.

As for the executive, he is well advised to look with caution on any company that tries to snap up managerial personnel by making outlandishly inflated bids for their services. Such firms are often acting in desperation, and the big money might not last.

There is a recent case in point that serves to illustrate how deadly booby traps may sometimes be attached to the most glittering offers.

A few years ago, a large and venerable corporation—which I shall call by the fictitious name of the De Sperate Company—underwent a drastic reorganization. De Sperate was engaged in publishing and other ventures, a corporate complex with a long history, huge and diversified assets and a fine reputation.

However, control of De Sperate passed from the numerous descendants and heirs of the founders to an outside group that decided on a drastic shake-up and installed a "fireball" executive at the top of the corporate pyramid.

After that, a great many things happened. First, the fireball did a wholesale housecleaning job, firing scores of De Sperate's veteran executives as well as hundreds of lesser employees. Then the company went on a large-scale executive-raiding campaign. Able managers employed by other firms were offered very high salaries and other glowing incentives to shift over to De Sperate. Among the many men approached was "Dan Miller," a friend of mine. During a conversation, he told me of the near-profligate offer he had received.

"Are you taking the job?" I asked.

"No, I'm not," Miller replied. "I smell a rat. The job simply isn't worth what the outfit is offering. The company is shopping around for far too many managers at the same time. I'm inclined to think there may be something wrong."

Miller admitted that all he had was a hunch. The fireball who had taken over top management of the corporate complex was widely reputed to be a miracle worker, and, after all, De Sperate was virtually a national institution.

Nonetheless, Dan Miller's suspicions proved to be well founded. The fireball flamed and sizzled, but whatever his previous qualifications and experience, by some fluke he proved totally incapable of heading an organization of De Sperate's particular type. Instead of showing greatly increased profits, the company lost money—millions each year. Other troubles developed: There were nasty internal squabbles. Costly projects proved to be total failures. Lawsuits of various kinds—involving staggering sums of money—were filed against the corporation.

And so it went, getting worse and worse, until the controlling group finally despaired and extinguished the fireball with a decision to send him packing before he burned the house down completely. Needless to say, many—in fact, according to reports, most—of the executives who had succumbed to the sky-high pay bait De Sperate offered during the fireball's tenure also found themselves without jobs. They went in the wake of his passing as the group in control of the corporation moved frantically to reduce costs, increase sales and profits —and clean out management personnel who had been brought in by the miracle worker, who had created only chaos.

Now, I do not mean to imply that a company that offers executives high pay is automatically suspect. Far from it. The case I have cited is an exceptional one. My purpose in narrating it is solely to suggest that while the astute and ambitious executive is entirely justified in looking out for his own financial welfare, he will also look beyond the dollars-and-cents price tag that is placed on a job.

According to the aforementioned survey, the fourth most common reason given for wanting to change jobs is disagreement with or objection to company policies. It is interesting to note that this was the reason advanced by the majority of company presidents among the respondents.

There are always liable to be differences of opinion among individuals engaged in any activity, and business is hardly an exception. Some differences can be resolved. Others can continue to exist but all concerned can live and work in peace despite them. However, when the differences are basic and serious and prevent an executive from working harmoniously, efficiently or in good conscience, he is wise indeed to express his regrets and tender his resignation.

Withal, it has been my experience that executives will make the decision to quit even the best of jobs for a wide variety of other, entirely valid reasons. For instance, a man may want to change his field, try his hand at some completely new type of managerial activity. Or, at a personal extreme of the scale, the health of a family member may dictate a change in job locales.

I recall an incident that occurred a few years ago in one of the companies in which I hold a substantial interest. An executive in the company —call him Bill Oliver—announced his intention to resign. Bill was a "comer," universally liked and highly regarded, a young man everyone agreed was headed for the top. We didn't want to lose him if we could possibly avoid it, and I took it upon myself to have a talk with Oliver. Curious to learn if he had some grievance or if there were some way he could be dissuaded from leaving, I asked Bill to tell me frankly the reasons for his decision.

"I have no complaints—none at all," he declared with what was obviously complete sincerity. "I like my job, the people I work with and the company itself and am entirely satisfied with my prospects. But, you see, I'm intrigued by the space industry. I won't be happy until I get into it, even if it means starting for less than I'm now making."

I grinned and gave up. I could understand how Bill Oliver felt. He had to move. He was irresistibly impelled to get into the space industry, which had captured his interest and fired his imagination. It would have been foolish to try to deter him.

Bill resigned and switched to a managerial job with a company producing space-vehicle components. I have since followed his career and have been gratified to note that he has been very successful, receiving several promotions so that he is now very near the top.

There is yet another important reason why some managers quit their jobs. It is a reason seldom discussed by organization-oriented management experts and personnel specialists—and more's the pity, for it involves the decision to stop being a salaried employee and to go into business for oneself.

Luckily for our economy, this still happens fairly often. Despite all the present-day emphasis on gaining "security" and the trend toward making a career in a large organization, there are still those individuals who prefer to achieve success on their own.

If I may be permitted to digress briefly, I have repeatedly expressed my belief that this is the only route to real success in the business world. Only by launching out on his own, building his own business, can an individual savor the full excitement and reap the greatest rewards that commerce and industry have to offer.

I think that when a man feels he is ready and equipped to go into business for himself, is cognizant of the risks involved and is willing to face them, he should unhesitatingly take the requisite giant step and make the most of his decision. Insofar as I am concerned, an executive in one of my companies who quits to start his own business does so with my full and sincere blessings and best wishes. In my opinion, such men provide the ever-needed fresh blood that ensures the health and the future of business and the entire free-enterprise system.

That said, and many of the reasons why executives quit having been discussed, it might be well to explore the questions of when and how an executive should go about leaving a job.

In these regards, there is no better guideline than that provided by the ancient gamblers' adage that holds that the wise player knows enough to quit when he is ahead of the game. The best time for an executive to quit a job is when he, too, is "ahead," in the sense that he has a good performance record and is well regarded in the company for which he is working.

Although I do not personally subscribe to many of the current theories and practices of executive "headhunting," I am realist enough to accept human nature for what it is and to acknowledge the harsher facts of business life. I am aware that, as Lawrence Stessin has observed in the *New York Times Magazine*, "it's an axiom of executive headhunting that to get a good job, one should already have a job."

This argument is echoed and amplified by C. R. Shelton and Melba Colgrove, writing in *Nation's Business*. The best time to resign, they advise, is "when you are in good standing with your firm. When you are unemployed, you are at a disadvantage in seeking employment," they warn. "Lack of a regular paycheck may lower your self-confidence. And being unemployed, for whatever reason, may render your judgment and your possible value to another firm suspect."

People are people, even when they're top-level managers who do the hiring for large organizations. And people are notoriously reluctant to take what they feel someone else has rejected. The fact that an executive is wanted by the company for which he works enhances his value and desirability.

When he quits, the wise manager also makes sure that he is ahead in his work, that he is not leaving any half-finished projects behind him. He knows that no matter how much his associates and superiors like him, they will deeply resent his leaving behind a mass of uncompleted work that others, who are totally unacquainted with it, will have to handle.

"We thought a lot of Smith around here. Then, after he quit, we discovered he hadn't bothered to tie up many loose ends. Consequently, his department was in a mess after his departure. It took his successor weeks to get things straightened out."

"Joe Howard left this company with glowing recommendations, and what a mistake that was! It later developed he'd been soldiering on the job for a month before he resigned, and none of his work was up to date. We lost two big accounts as a result."

Word travels fast and far in business circles. Remarks such as these can play havoc with a man's future prospects. The wise executive makes certain they cannot be made about him after he leaves a company.

Age is another factor that should be taken into consideration when deciding to quit or not to quit. "Most companies seek men between forty and fifty for top-management jobs," Chester Burger states. "For middle management, the preferred age level

115

is between thirty and forty."

C. R. Shelton and Melba Colgrove quote Harold K. Daniels, vice-president of Parke, Davis: "At least by the time you approach forty, you should have found yourself and have most of your job moves behind you."

I'm not sure that I would accept these generalizations as Holy Writ. Some men are outstanding top-management material long before they reach 40—and, conversely, some of the best, most solid and seasoned middle-management personnel are well beyond Chester Burger's "preferred" 40-year limit. And I've known more than a few executives who made several big upward steps when they were in their mid-40s or even considerably older. Nevertheless, I imagine that with appropriate allowances for individual cases or special situations, the Burger and Shelton-Colgrove generalizations do serve as fairly reliable rules of thumb.

As for the question of *how* an executive should go about quitting, the answer, in my opinion, is very simple: He should do it frankly and honestly, giving proper notice and always writing a letter of resignation. He should state his reasons for resigning clearly and succinctly, but avoiding any personal recriminations.

This advice is not only good manners, it is also good business practice. Nothing leaves a worse taste in management's mouth than the man who quits without warning or explanation, who simply fails to show up in the morning or announces that he is through a few minutes before the office closes on Friday afternoon. It is also sound practice to quit without letting off steam, without taking the last-minute opportunity to tell this or that person where to head in.

These are cheap and cowardly tricks that have a habit of boomeranging on those who resort to them. I know of many cases like that of pseudonymous Ted Spencer, who quietly obtained a job with another company and then, on a Friday afternoon—needless to say, *after* he'd received his paycheck—loudly told off his superior and announced that he was quitting then and there.

No doubt Ted Spencer derived a certain amount of personal satisfaction from his dramatic little act, but he was destined to regret it intensely. About a year and a half later, Spencer's old company absorbed the one to which he'd moved—and, lo and behold, the superior Ted had berated became his boss again. That is, he became Ted's boss for about a week—which was all the time it took for Spencer to find himself unemployed.

All in all, quitting rules are really not much different from any other rules of sound human conduct. Each man must decide for himself when it's quitting time, when it is advisable and advantageous for him to leave a job and a company and move elsewhere. Once he has decided to resign, he should take the step in a clean, straightforward fashion.

In short, the wise business executive emulates the wise gambler and quits when he is ahead. Beyond this, he bears in mind that sometimes it is necessary to quit in order to get ahead and that the man who knows when to quit is often the one who gets ahead the fastest and the farthest.

8.
THE MYTH OF THE ORGANIZATION MAN

THAT CORPORATE STEREOTYPE
OF THE BLAND LEADING THE BLAND
DOESN'T EXIST—AND FOR GOOD REASON

I imagine that almost everyone is familiar with the age-old, perennially popular game "Bait the Businessman." But for the benefit of those who, by some freak of fate, have remained ignorant of the game, permit me to describe its rudimentary form.

Any number—from one to millions—can play. There are no rules—or, rather, as long as the player remembers to derogate businessmen for selfishness, misdeeds and effronteries, the player can make his own rules. Beginners may improve their technique by studying the effusions of professional coaches, such as the German socialist August Bebel, whose 19th Century handbook recommends such classic opening gambits as, "The nature of all business is swindling."

I do not intend to topple the towers of Bebel or to battle other *aficionados* of the game. My immediate concern is with a much-refined version of the original sport that has gained favor in recent years. Unlike the parent pastime, the objective of this variant is not to tar and feather businessmen but to dress them in the drab cloak of conformity. There are two ways to score points: One is by maintaining that a business career is a deadly bore, a rat race or a soul destroyer (select one or coin your own). The other is by steadfastly averring that businessmen are dull, achromatic creatures devoid of initiative, creativity and courage.

Bonus points are awarded for negative characterizations couched in the heliotrope prose of the dead gray-flannel-suit days. For example, a player would be assured of an upper-division rating if he declared, "Businessmen are faceless automatons plodding seriatim through the deepest grooves of organization, constantly glancing over their shoulders in fear, unfeelingly trampling the bodies of their fellows who fall by the wayside."

Of course, I reject the contention that business is boring. For those who enthusiastically decide to make it their career, business offers challenge, excitement and risks galore—as much of each as any man could desire or handle. "Business *is* an adventure," John Brooks has written, and the emphasis is his.

Take, for example, the romance of the oil business, which is the business I know best. Its romance is reflected even in the normally dry-as-dust legal precedents that govern the industry. Many years ago, American courts established the legal concept of the "law of capture," ruling that oil is like the

121

wild animal in the jungle: It belongs to the man who finds and captures it. The analogy between oil and jungle beast can be carried considerably further. Both are elusive, unpredictable and frequently dangerous. Although it is possible on rare occasions to stumble across either unwittingly, in the vast majority of instances both must be hunted down with patience, brought to bay with caution and subdued swiftly. Furthermore, both oilmen and big-game hunters are likely to range over remote and forbidding regions in search of their prey, facing great hardships in the process.

Excitement in business? I remember one incident—by no means unique in my experience—when, in 1923, my father's Nordstrom well, located in a southern-California field, blew out. For days, every effort had to be concentrated on extinguishing the roaring blaze—which melted structural steel as though it were butter—before the flames spread to adjacent wells and storage tanks. This could have caused a major disaster. Believe me, once you fight a few conflagrations like that, you have tasted high adventure.

Parenthetically, there's an amusing sidelight to this story. The Nordstrom well was situated only 150 yards or so from the Santa Fe railroad tracks. When the well blew and it became obvious that we had a serious fire on our hands, I hastened to telephone the traffic superintendent of the Santa Fe in Los Angeles. I told him what had happened and warned him to stop all rail traffic along the line. Any trains passing through would be in grave danger.

The Santa Fe official—possibly thinking I was some sort of crank—got his hackles up and refused to halt or reroute traffic on my say-so. Fortunately, however, he decided to make an independent check. One of the railroad's employees made a quick visit to the scene. I called the superintendent back a little while later, for the fire was getting worse, and repeated my urgent request.

"Yeah, I know," he growled dourly. "You really do have a fire—traffic's been stopped all along the line." With that, he hung up, a very unhappy traffic superintendent.

There may or may not be close parallels to emergencies such as oil-well fires in other industrial and commercial spheres; nonetheless, the drama of business extends across a very broad spectrum. I shall have more to say on this later, but for the moment let us turn our attention to the businessman and seek to determine whether he is as drab as some hold him to be.

Now, I do not deny that there are archconformists, yes-men and Caspar Milquetoasts to be found in the business community. You will find these types in *any* community. Such men do not require others to dress them in the 1971 equivalent of a gray flannel suit; they don the cloak of conformity voluntarily, as camouflage, hoping to blend into a background of mediocrity, because they are insecure, incompetent and in the wrong field. Decades of observation and experience have led me to believe they are the persons least likely to succeed in the business world.

Interviewed not long ago by *Nation's Business,* Walter E. Heller, head of the large commercial finance company that bears his name, was asked, "What do you think are the major skills and qualities that today's manager needs?"

"The two things he has to have or he doesn't make the grade are courage and vision," Heller replied. "Those are the sheer essentials."

Who will get the promotions and the best jobs? According to Paul H. Kiernan, managing director of the international recruiting firm of Kiernan and Company, it will not be the bland conformist but "the man with vision and enough guts to change things."

These are only two samplings from the vast number of similar assessments made by individuals who, having reached the summit the hard way, are in an excellent position to speak. Clearly and unanimously, the qualities they cite as "musts" for success are the absolute antitheses of those implied by the Milquetoast cliché. And the higher the individual climbs up the slopes of the business world's Annapurnas, the headier is the atmosphere and the greater the attendant risks and the concomitant needs for creativity and individuality.

In their incisive and valuable study *The Managers*, Roy Lewis and Rosemary Stewart argue that "the man who founds a successful business is still likely to be . . . aggressive" and will see "his company as a tangible projection of himself. He seldom wears the mask of modesty that is standard for the corporation man."

Dissecting successful businessmen in his book *The Multimillionaires*, Goronwy Rees contends that the man who passes the magic million mark, "in addition to being a calculator, patient, thorough and scrupulous in his regard for fact, however distasteful, [is] a gambler on a colossal scale."

Rees continues, "It is the willingness to accept . . . huge risks that psychologically distinguishes the multimillionaire, in his classical form as an individual entrepreneur backing his judgment with his own resources, from his fellowmen and even from those very rich men whose abilities are employed within the framework of great joint-stock companies and corporations."

Rees provides many illustrative examples to support his theorems, including an anecdote about my good friend and recent headline maker Aristotle Onassis: "When Mr. Onassis first proposed to build a tanker of 60,000 tons, he was regarded by the banks . . . as a dreamer of the most impractical kind; and, indeed, he says he was able to do it only by concealing from everyone the size of the giant he proposed to build."

Of course, Ari's dream has long since proved thoroughly practical. Oil tankers much larger than 60,000 tons are now sliding down the ways of shipyards all over the world. Nevertheless, Rees renders Ari Onassis a well-deserved salute by commenting, "Such actions might not provoke surprise if carried out by huge corporations; [but] on the part of an individual, they involve a degree of risk that can affect his entire fortune."

I myself am hardly a stranger to such risks. Like many other businessmen, I have frequently found it advisable to take them during the course of my career. Such was the case when I began my campaign to gain control of the Tide Water Associated Oil Company in the depression years of the 1930s. It was unquestionably a gamble and, by my standards, it was an enormous one. I was then a relatively small wildcatting operator setting my sights on one of the nation's major oil companies. My stock purchases were financed by every dollar

125

I possessed and every cent of credit I could obtain. Had I lost the campaign (and I was defeated in several preliminary skirmishes and came within heart-stopping hairbreadths of total failure on several occasions), I would have been left personally penniless and very deeply in debt. However, the campaign was a success. By 1940, Getty interests held 1,734,577 shares of Tide Water—about one-fourth of the voting stock. The company was recently merged into the Getty Oil Company. The market value of this holding is now well over one billion dollars.

At least an equal degree of risk was involved when I authorized the purchase of a Middle Eastern oil concession for $12.5 million—cash in advance—before anyone was certain there was a drop of oil to be found anywhere in the area covered by the concession. Years would pass and many more millions of dollars would be invested before the first producing well would come in. Had there not been oil in the area—well, I'd just as soon not even think about *that* possibility.

All in all, it is my opinion that the Dullsville image of the businessman fits only a very small, notably unsuccessful segment of the business community. I have observed that the suave, superconformist éminence grise of the executive suite is mainly a mythical creature. As I noted, I will grant that the species *does* exist, but its members are few and they seldom attain suiteworthy rank. If they enter the board room at all, the chances are it is only to set out the writing pads or to empty the ashtrays.

I contend that the individualist—the man who risks unmarked roads and takes a great many hard

126

knocks en route—possesses an immense advantage over any conformist, organization type. My views on this subject began to form as far back as 1914, when I started my own career as a businessman in the oil fields of Oklahoma.

In those days, I lived at the Cordova Hotel in Tulsa (rent: six dollars per week) and took my meals at a boardinghouse close by (weekly board bill: another six dollars). Several men destined to become millionaires shared the table at the boardinghouse. Among them was my close friend R. A. Josey, whose nature and personality were the opposite of what would be considered standard for the typical organization man. "Josie," as he was predictably nicknamed, was a complete individualist, and although he later became a very wealthy man, he remained the same person—good-natured, self-reliant and resilient, as far a cry as one could imagine from the achromatic stereotype.

Many other friends and acquaintances of that period preveniently refuted the myth of the bland businessman and, in fact, seemed to demonstrate that the more multihued an individual's character, the better his chances for achieving success. Certainly their careers proved that imagination, initiative and resiliency are infinitely more valuable assets than the ability to fit into a mold, to move with the crowd or to allow the judgment of others to influence one's own actions.

For instance, I am sure that many people would have insisted that R. M. McFarlin was finished when he failed in the cattle business; they would have doubtless advised him to seek safe and steady employment and to forget about trying to make a fortune. But, undaunted by failure, McFarlin went to Oklahoma and started over and became the multimillionaire part owner of the McMan Oil Company, one of the country's most successful oil-producing enterprises.

Then there was Bill Roeser, who, though then not yet 30, had made—and lost—two or three fortunes. In 1914 he was in the process of making yet another fortune. He habitually sported a $10,000 bill as a boutonniere, to advertise that he was on his way up again. Marion L. Travis, then only 28, had started on the slenderest shoestring only a few years before and made millions. John Markham, ignoring the advice of the "experts," followed his own instincts and took what the consensus held to be a sure step to bankruptcy by buying the unproved Sarah Rector Lease on the northern edge of the Cushing Field in Oklahoma. John knew it was a gamble, but he won. After the first well was drilled (it came in a gusher), the property proved to be one of the richest in the state. It made John Markham a multimillionaire.

Oddly enough, I had an experience almost identical to Markham's a short time later. Throughout Oklahoma, it was virtually an article of faith that no oil could exist in the so-called red-beds area. Without exception, geologists, major-oil-company experts and wildcatting operators agreed that the region was bone-dry. I wasn't so sure. In fact, I had a strong hunch that the unanimous opinion was based on nothing more than superstition and guesswork. The hunch was bolstered by the information that only the most haphazard and desultory exploration had been carried out in the red beds. I therefore decided to take a very big risk. I obtained a lease in the region, began drilling and opened up a new producing area. Thenceforth, to put it mildly, I no longer needed to live at the Cordova or to eat at the boardinghouse.

The roster of colorful, individualistic and notably successful businessmen I have known throughout the years could be extended far beyond the space of this article. Suffice it to say that these men achieved their successes in many different spheres of industry and commerce and that all had traits that set them apart from the herd. Foremost among these qualities was that each was a distinctive personality—each was fearlessly himself, not what he thought others might want him to be. Almost all had taken many hard knocks on their way to the top, and each and every one possessed the courage and vision that Walter Heller called the sheer essentials for success.

Notwithstanding cant and claptrap to the contrary, the operative human factors haven't changed. The same characteristics that proved decisive in the past are still adding that extra thrust that distinguishes a moderate achievement from an outstanding business success.

There is more challenge, adventure and opportunity than ever before in the business world for young men who have courage and vision, who are able to roll with the punches and recover from them quickly and who are willing to disregard all they have ever heard about the organization-man myth. One needs only to glance over published reports to sense the climate of unparalleled opportunity and to realize the exhilaration (to say nothing of the financial rewards) that accrues to those who seize their chances.

In 1968, the Internal Revenue Service estimated

that there were 100,000 millionaires in the United States—an astounding 150-percent increase over 1958, when there were 40,000 in the millionaire category. (A millionaire, of course, is a person whose possessions would realize one million dollars or more if they were sold.) However one studies the IRS figures, they are phenomenal—and extremely heartening to one who argues, as I have been doing for decades, that the American free-enterprise system is neither dying nor ailing and that its future is more promising than its past or its present. What I find especially encouraging about the multiplication of millionaires is that a very considerable percentage of the new arrivals is comprised of young men.

The successes achieved by individuals in their early 40s, their 30s or even their 20s has been widely publicized. For example, when *Time* devoted a cover story to the younger generation of millionaires in America, it profiled several men who began with little or no capital but managed to become millionaires before they reached 40. These successful businessmen of the 1960s had amassed their fortunes in a wide range of enterprise—from real estate and electronics to show business and presqueezed orange juice. All, said *Time*, "built productive wealth by creating jobs, purchasing power and useful ideas. . . . [They] realize that even a million-dollar idea is useless unless the man who has it knows how to put it to work and has the courage to take risks."

There are hundreds, even thousands, of such young men among America's more than 60,000 new millionaires.

How did they do it? The answer is simple: in

precisely the same way as their predecessors. They had the vision to recognize the commercial potential for certain products or services and, having the courage of their convictions, addressed themselves to the task of realizing that potential.

A definitive summation can be found in the published statement of youthful entrepreneur Robert K. Lifton, who, speaking of businessmen and their drive to succeed, declared, "This is our form of creating. If artists give up the world's pleasures to pursue their calling, people understand it. What they don't understand is that many businessmen have the same creative drives and derive the same satisfactions as artists—but what they are doing is translated into dollars and cents. When I come up with a good deal, that's creative. Successfully merchandising a product is creative. Taking a business idea and making it work is creative."

Young men who want to make a career of business will find nothing drab or boring about industry and commerce. They will find their work as invigorating and as exhilarating as any they could imagine. They will confront the challenge of the marketplace and feel the thrill and the satisfaction that come from business creativity.

Despite all the efforts of their detractors, it is simply not possible to color such men gray or any other shade of drabness. Exceptionally successful businessmen are not men who have been fitted in standardized slots; each is a man unique unto himself. The dowdy vestments of conformity and mediocrity can never be tailored to fit such men or their philosophies, no matter how their critics may tug in their efforts to shape the cloth.

I anticipate—indeed, I confidently prophesy—

that there will be an even greater multiplication of young millionaires in the next few years. And it would not surprise me in the least if, as their number increases, their average age decreases.

Yes, by all means, let him who, for whatever reason, scorns a business career go in peace to find his rightful place wherever else he wishes. I most sincerely wish him good fortune in whatever field he chooses. On the other hand, if he wants to be a businessman, he should not permit the businessman baiters to discourage him. He should take his priceless assets of vision and courage and head for the peak.

9.
SAYING NO
TO THE
YES MENTALITY

**UNLESS HE'S WISE
TO THE MORES OF MANAGEMENT,
THE ASPIRING EXECUTIVE
MAY LEARN THE HARD WAY
THAT POLISHING
JUST SOURS
THE APPLE**

The president of a medium-sized company in which I held a substantial interest once found himself hopelessly overburdened with work, due to the implementation of an expansion program. The company president—let's call him Edward Blaine —decided to hire an assistant. He thought a capable aide could relieve him of much onerous and time-consuming detail, keep an eye on minor routine matters and act as a sort of buffer and sifter. Blaine reasoned that with such help he would be able to better concentrate on the many major problems confronting his company.

Ed Blaine interviewed several prescreened and promising applicants. He finally settled on "Walter

Thomas," a young man who seemed to show intelligence, drive and ambition and who gave every indication of possessing the ability to quickly grasp and efficiently handle the work expected of him. Thomas, in short, appeared to be a happy answer to a harried president's prayer.

But appearances can be deceiving, and they certainly were in this instance. Walter Thomas's career as assistant to the president lasted less than three months; he was sacked—and with good reason.

Some time later, during the course of a general conversation that led to a discussion of personnel matters, Ed Blaine glumly recounted the incident to me. "Thomas proved to be one of *those* personnel errors," Blaine began, scowling at the recollection. "I hired him to take some of the load off my back, and the next thing I knew, I had far more work than before and far less time in which to do it."

Ed went on to describe a type of executive and the situations he creates that are unfortunately familiar to upper-level managers. By all outwardly measurable standards, Walter Thomas had been an entirely satisfactory choice. He *did* possess potentials and qualifications that fitted him for the position he was hired to fill. The trouble was that Thomas's weaknesses evidenced themselves only after he started on the job. It was then that his true nature came to the fore. He simply could not use his abilities constructively; his drive and ambition were directed to unproductive and purely self-seeking channels. Instead of performing the tasks at hand, he constantly gave performances intended solely to flatter and impress his superior. Walter Thomas was—to employ a charitable euphemism

135

—an apple-polisher, born and bred, quite beyond salvation.

"He'd come into my office a dozen times each day, soft-soaping me until I gagged, constantly asking my advice and acting as though I were omniscience personified whenever I gave it," Blaine related disgustedly. "In between these sessions, he'd dictate mountains of memorandums—all addressed to me, naturally. He did everything but the work he was supposed to do, trying to convince me he was slaving to the point of exhaustion but doing it gladly because I was such a great guy."

Neither fool nor vainglorious egoist, Edward Blaine was singularly unimpressed by his assistant's tactics. When a blunt and vigorous reeducational cram course failed to have any effect, he sent the young man and his overworked polishing cloth packing.

Walter Thomas was by no means the first of his ilk to find the boot he'd sought to lick being firmly planted in his gluteal region and propelling him out the door. Strangely enough, no matter how badly bruised their posteriors, such types continue to crop up in almost all business organizations. They refuse to believe the basic truths that may be boiled down into a slightly muddled but nonetheless axiomatic metaphor that overpolishing the apple will create sufficient friction to remove its protective peel.

Like any individual who has achieved any degree of authority in the business world, I have encountered my share of toadies who sought to gain attention through flattery. However, while their numbers are considerable and the energy they expend is great, their successes in achieving their goals are few. It has been my observation that such individuals are predestined to fail because they almost invariably make several major mistakes.

First of all, they are too eager for quick results. Hence, they employ what they consider the most potent, quickest-acting stratagems, which, 99 times out of 100, are so unsubtle and maladroit that they are completely transparent.

Second, the devoted apple-polisher is so intent on his truckling and favor currying that he neglects his official duties. Any superior who has reached an upper-level position in the hardheaded, competitive world of business has done so only because he possesses an objective outlook. He judges a subordinate's performance on the basis of results achieved. No amount of bootlicking will compensate for inadequacies found in the profit-and-loss statement.

Third—and this comes close to being an ultimate absurdity—the dedicated apple-polisher is, like Walter Thomas, often a fundamentally intelligent and able individual with considerable potential. Were he to devote as much time and effort to productive work as he does to playing the slavering spaniel, he would advance much faster. And, what is more, he would in the process gain, rather than lose, the respect of those above him.

Fourth, most seasoned businessmen have long since learned the hard way that there is more than a grain of truth in George Herbert's acid adage, "Many kiss the hand they wish cut off." The scarred veteran of business battles is all too aware that the apple-polisher is quite often a completely cynical opportunist—a sneak who seeks to ingratiate himself in order to make it easier for him to stab in the back those he flatters. Consequently, and if for no other reason, superiors are alert for signs of servile adulation. Whenever they recognize any such signs, they are instantly suspicious. Thus, the sycophant who briskly applies his polishing cloth is more often than not earning distrust rather than approbation.

It is, indeed, deplorable that some still believe otherwise, maintaining that principles such as those I've just set forth are fine in theory but not valid in practice. The basis for such arguments rests on the familiar contentions that "everyone likes flattery" and "all human beings enjoy being made to feel important." To make matters even worse for those who pay them heed, some "experts" are even wont to advise young executives that elbow grease expended in shining apples will carry them a long way down the road to success.

Permit me to cite an example, quoting from Victor A. Thompson's book *Modern Organization,* in which the author writes, "Subordinates must create the impression that they *need* to be told what to do; that they *need* to be told how to do it; and, in general, that they could not get along without the boss." (The italics are Mr. Thompson's.) So far, so good—or so bad.

However, somewhat farther along—and with what I consider striking inconsistency—Mr. Thompson declares, "Since the superior is presented as the busiest and most important person, subordinates must create the impression that they understand that he has little time to deal with them." And even farther along, "Many subordinates, therefore, attempt communication with the boss infrequently and briefly. . . . Subordinates must create the impression that they feel awed and humble in his presence."

With all due respect to the author, I wish I could reconcile what I find to be glaring contradictions in these statements. At first he sounds as though he is counseling executives to mercilessly pester their superiors, constantly ask them for orders and beg for detailed directions. Then, inexplicably, Mr. Thompson does an abrupt *volte-face*, apparently advising these same executives to leave their superiors (who have "little time to deal with them") pretty much alone. Finally, again abruptly changing his tack, he implies that the superior is to be treated with "awe" by "humble" subordinates.

Beyond finding these arguments to be contrary to all I have experienced in business, I cannot follow the fractured logic the author employs. But, then, I have noticed that this same sort of tortuous and totally unconvincing reasoning characterizes all the arguments I have heard in favor of seeking success through flattery.

Now, I do not claim to know all there is to know about the business world—far from it. Although I have been a businessman for more than 50 years, I do not exaggerate one whit when I say that I have learned, and still learn, something new about business every day. Nevertheless, I believe I have had enough business experience to know, and to state flatly, that in the great majority of industrial and commercial organizations, the fawning time-server is not only at the top of the expendable list but is usually quickly expended.

I have very little patience with the carpers who delight in characterizing businessmen and top executives as insecure, vainglorious nincompoops who would wither and die unless fed a steady diet of adulation by their subordinates. Occasional exceptions aside—and one can find exceptions to even the hardest rule—it simply isn't so.

The tempo and complexity of modern business, the heavy and continuing pressures on every executive at every level and the very nature of "organization" as we know it in business today are only a few factors that utterly demolish any "bootlick your way to success" myth.

Theory versus practice? All right. Let us look briefly at the workaday truths and harsh operational realities that prove decisive in modern commerce and industry.

In our present highly competitive, rapidly and constantly changing era, businessmen have to be tough, practical and realistic in order to survive. The fundamental factors that tip the scales—to success or to failure—are self-evident and sharply defined:

1. A company either makes a profit or it does not.

2. An office or department either operates and produces efficiently or it does not.

3. An executive either does his job properly or he does not. If he fails to perform his duties and discharge his responsibilities in a satisfactory fashion—in making adequate contributions toward the achievement of the positive alternatives cited above—he is out. And no degree of venality or sycophancy will be likely to keep his neck off the corporate chopping block.

Frankly, I would like to meet the successful president or upper-echelon executive of a successful company who cares more about his subordinates' kowtows than he does about his production costs. If such men and companies exist, then the stockholders thereof would be well advised to run, not walk, to the nearest brokerage house to unload their shares. The companies will not remain successful. Pride, it is said, goes before a fall. The high cost of feeding what Carlyle has described as "the sixth, insatiable sense" of a vain top manager will swiftly plunge any organization into a sea of red ink.

Take it from me or, if you prefer, from just about every leading member of the business community I've ever met—there is mighty little room in business for either the man who wants his subordinates to be bootlickers or the man who is willing to do the licking. Either type is definitely *non grata* and a liability no thriving company can afford.

Until now, I have approached my theme from a largely negative standpoint. I have hoped thus to impress my readers with the folly inherent in seeking business success through the flattering of superiors. I have touched upon positive aspects of the issue only by implication. Consequently, I believe it might be worthwhile to do my own version of an about-face and examine a few of what I have found and observed to be explicit positive pointers.

To begin with, every young executive must realize there is a very clear distinction between what I have labeled apple-polishing and the common courtesy and respect a subordinate may reasonably be expected to show a superior.

For the sake of argument, let us accept the slightly unorthodox theory postulated in the *Jour-*

nal of Business by Robert Tannenbaum, who holds that authority stems from two sources. The first, which he calls "formal," originates "at the top of an organization hierarchy" and flows "downward therein through the process of delegation." The second, or "informal," source of the authority "possessed by an individual lies in the acceptance of its exercise by those who are subject to it," Tannenbaum says.

Whatever the source, the young executive must appreciate that his superior *does* have authority and that, all things being equal, it is accepted by others. As a junior, he is also required to accept that authority if he wishes to become a functioning member of the organization. It's entirely possible that the young executive might not personally like his superior, but the courtesy and respect due the latter are not necessarily based on any personal considerations. They are due, if for no other reason, because the superior has had considerably more experience than the junior; he has "been through the mill" and demonstrated his abilities. It is highly unlikely that the junior possesses anywhere near the seasoning of the superior. The former has much to learn, and the latter has much to teach him.

Here, again, we face a distinction—this time between legitimate requests for guidance from a superior and constant, unnecessary pleas for advice intended solely to feed the superior's ego and draw his attention to the adulation with which the junior regards him. Any boss worthy of the title will gladly give constructive counsel and assistance to a subordinate, for he knows that only thus will the subordinate realize his full potential. On the other hand, that same boss will not tolerate a subordinate who tags constantly at his heels, besieging him with needless questions and requests.

There is one reliable test a subordinate can apply to determine whether or not he's overstepping the line in this regard. Whenever he has a problem he is tempted to take to the boss, he should ask himself the following questions:

"Am I sure I can't answer this myself within the limits of my area of authority? Or, if I can't do it myself immediately, are there sources from which I can obtain the necessary information without 'going upstairs'?"

Only after exhausting all other available avenues should the junior go to the boss. A competent, mature senior executive will unquestionably award far more points for displays of initiative and self-reliance than he will for being bothered endlessly over trivial matters.

Straining to impress superiors with how long and how hard they are working is among the most common—and most transparent and annoying—tactics misguided subordinates employ to attract attention and curry favor. This hoary ploy seldom accomplishes much beyond irritating the boss, who can probably top any of his subordinates in hours of time and ergs of energy expended in doing his job.

The surest way the young executive can prove that he's really straining and thus gain approbation is by concentrating on his work, carrying out the tasks assigned to him and achieving whatever goals have been set for the activity under his control. Let him increase production, reduce costs, carry out his part of a program efficiently and on—or ahead of—schedule or otherwise give concrete evidence that he has worked hard and he won't have to point any fingers at himself to be noticed. His accomplishments will flash all the signals and sound all the bells necessary to make the boss take notice.

Heaping praise on a superior's head is another familiar gambit used by soft-soap artists. Now, I do not intend to suggest that a subordinate should invariably avoid making any laudatory comment to his superior. Far from it, for there is nothing improper about passing complimentary remarks, subject to the results of a preliminary test:

Is praise justified from two standpoints: Has the superior really accomplished something warranting praise and, if so, is the subordinate qualified, and is it within his province, to pass judgment on it?

How often does the subordinate take it upon himself to give the boss a pat on the back? Does he do it only when it is appropriate or habitually, grabbing at every opportunity to applaud his chief's actions? What is the manner in which the subordinate does the praising—is it simple, straightforward and sincere or is it treacly, grandiloquent and abased?

The right answers to these questions should be evident to even the tyro, and only if all the answers are right in any given situation should a subordinate express praise.

While we're on the subject of praising the boss, we might also consider the question of criticizing him. Situations—sometimes crucial ones—do occasionally arise when a subordinate has ample justification to criticize his superior. To refrain from doing so under such conditions is a passive, but still pernicious, form of apple-polishing. How should a subordinate proceed? I can add nothing to the excellent advice William B. Given, Jr., chairman of American Brake Shoe Company, gave in a *Nation's Business* article.

"How do you criticize the boss?" he wrote. "A realistic answer: In about the same manner as you yourself would want to be criticized by a subordinate. Nobody particularly enjoys criticism. Yet, if you feel something the boss is doing or failing to do cramps your performance or that of someone else in your department, this means it is cramping his performance, too. You should be able to find an acceptable way to discuss it with him. Actually, this is not so difficult as it may seem; he may take it as a compliment that you feel free to criticize. If you are in doubt, do it."

I agree wholeheartedly with Mr. Given. A good executive—regardless of how high he is on the organization chart—will listen to justified constructive criticism that is properly presented. He knows that he is not infallible, that he can make mistakes that might cramp an individual's or a department's performance and that eventually this will adversely affect not only his own performance but the welfare of the company as well. In the vast majority of cases, he will be grateful to have the error called to his attention and will gain respect for the subordinate who did the calling.

Returning to the mainstream of my discourse, an executive can avoid the perils of rubbing the peel from his career apple fairly easily. A sense of proportion and equilibrium and, above all, plain common sense are his principal defenses.

Any man who imagines himself a manager

145

should start off on a job or career acutely conscious that an executive's purpose in business life is to help achieve company goals—not to become a teacher's pet to his superior.

Even though he might be the rawest beginner and a basket case insofar as common sense is concerned, he should—if nothing else—bear in mind that the superior whose favor and favoritism he curries may be shifted to another department, or leave the company, at any time. The departed superior's successor is not very likely to look with much sympathy upon a subordinate who has already labeled himself a toady.

But men with wider intellectual vistas and sounder perspectives are aware that, to succeed in any position of responsibility, an executive must work *with* people, and this most certainly includes those who are his equals. Furthermore, they know that the rule works both ways—if they are to accomplish anything at all, people must work with them.

Whether equals or subordinates, people are singularly unenthusiastic about working with anyone who is working solely for himself and only toward the goal of becoming the boss's *enfant gâté*. They will regard him with distaste and resentment—let us view human nature and human reactions with realistic honesty—and they will not find it difficult to contrive and spring a wide variety of deadly traps to rid themselves of his presence.

All things considered, I would hardly say that the executive who tries to truckle his way to the top has a very promising future in the business world. Even if men like these are lucky, the most they can look forward to is wedging themselves into some lower-middle-management slot and remaining there long enough to qualify for retirement benefits.

In my opinion, the executives most likely to succeed in business are self-made—in the sense that they rely on their own abilities and hard work to fuel their journey up the ladder. They disdain any thought of attaching themselves to vainglorious "patron" superiors. They would never dream of playing puppet or constantly scraping and applauding in an effort to ingratiate themselves with the boss.

The best men are those who would rather forgo personal benefit or even promotion than sacrifice their self-respect. They earn their promotions, and in the process they also earn the respect of others. On the other hand, the confirmed apple-polisher seldom gains anything but contempt wherever he goes. True, if he persists in his habit energetically enough, he might well achieve one—albeit unplanned and unwelcome—result: He might polish off his entire business career. It is even possible for him to wind up applying his well-worn polishing cloth to the apples on a corner fruit stand!

10.
GYPS
THAT PASS
IN THE NIGHT

HOW THE EXECUTIVE
CAN THREAD HIS WAY THROUGH
A FINANCIAL LANDSCAPE MINED
WITH DOLLAR-DIVESTING CHICANERY

have been in business a long time, and I've seen a sizable chunk of the business world. It has been my experience that the majority of businessmen are honest and that they conduct their business affairs honestly, adhering to the spirit as well as the letter of the law.

Nonetheless, one is liable to encounter cheats and frauds in the business world just as he is liable to encounter them anywhere. There are always some individuals in every sector of commerce and industry who cut corners, seek out the loopholes in the laws and engage in unethical or even illegal practices. They are, however, in the minority, and the great mass of legitimate businessmen would dearly love to be rid of them.

But, obviously, the world in which we live is hardly utopian. Everyone—be he taxi driver or tycoon—has to be on his guard to avoid being cheated in the marketplace by the small but ubiquitous percentage of unethical or dishonest businessmen.

I received my introduction to these more dismal facts of business life early in my career, when I began wildcatting for oil in Oklahoma. The great Oklahoma oil rush was a magnet that drew highbinders, swindlers and plain, ordinary crooks as well as honest, hardworking men to the drilling sites and boom towns. Land pirates, credit sharks, confidence men and manipulators of all kinds were among those who flocked to the oil fields. Fraudulent leases, bogus deeds, worthless stocks—these were only a few of the devices the swindlers employed to mulct money from the unwary and gullible. Countless people were fleeced in one way or another by the sharpsters.

Among the most vicious forms of fraud was the fatal credit trap that crooked "grubstakers" and unscrupulous equipment dealers set for wildcatting operators who held leases on promising properties.

"Take all the equipment and gear you need. Just sign this paper" was the siren song chanted by the credit sharks. "We trust you. The paper is a mere formality."

The wildcatter who signed received all the credit he needed—until he brought in a producing well. Then the vultures who held his notes would descend and take over his lease and equipment, leaving him little but the clothes he wore.

One of my acquaintances fell into such a trap.

151

Holding the lease on a property he felt certain would prove to bear oil, he went to a credit shark. Signing the agreements that were thrust under his nose, he purchased everything he needed to drill a test well—on credit. He spudded his well and a few weeks later struck oil. The man who held his notes immediately called them in and seized the wildcatter's lease and rig. To his sorrow, the wildcatter learned he had no recourse; the fine-print clauses in the agreements he had signed gave his creditor the right to do as he pleased. The gyp eventually netted a $250,000 profit on the lease he literally stole.

The most regrettable aspect of such incidents was that there was absolutely no need for them to happen. For every credit shark operating in the oil fields, there were two legitimate machinery-and-equipment firms who would grubstake and extend credit to independent operators. I myself occasionally found I was short of capital and had to buy machinery and equipment on credit. I never encountered any undue difficulty in obtaining what I needed on fair terms from reputable dealers. I, like many other successful oilmen, willingly concede that I owe at least part of my success to the help I received from the legitimate machinery-and-equipment dealers who grubstaked me at various times during the early stages of my career.

There were also other avenues open to the wildcatter who was short of cash. Banks and individuals with capital to spare would finance exploration and drilling operations at fair rates of interest or in return for reasonable shares in a venture.

Why, then, didn't all independent operators obtain their financing from legitimate sources? The reasons are many, varied *and* familiar. In the first place, the credit sharks talked fast and made everything seem ever so easy and attractive. They seldom mentioned such sordid details as interest rates or the method of repayment. On the other hand, reputable dealers clearly stated the terms on which they would grant credit; they made no pretense of giving anything away free. They also took a bit more time to think things over than did the sharks, who grabbed eagerly at any proposition, for they knew they could afford almost any risks on their immense profit margins.

Then, some wildcatters had an instinctive distrust of banks and bankers. Their concept of a banker was of a gimlet-eyed, rapacious plunderer of widows and orphans—a totally erroneous idea, but one unfortunately still held by many.

The cruelhearted, cold-blooded banker is a good "heavy" character for cheap cowboy films, but that's about all. The average banker is a man who is in business to help his clients, be they depositors or borrowers. He must safeguard the interests of the former and supply the needs of the latter. That's the only way he can stay in the banking business.

Still other independents were reluctant to surrender any share of their anticipated profits in return for the financing of their operations. Instead of agreeing to part with a 25- or 30-percent share, they went to the credit cheats, who said they wanted nothing, but in the end took everything.

The credit sharks are still with us today. They victimize the general public as well as the small businessman—and sometimes businessmen who are not so small. A while back, a Senate banking subcommittee heard evidence of how these gyps operate. The subcommittee members listened to a dismal recital of sharp, usurious and unethical loan and credit practices. There was testimony that some so-called small-loan companies, automobile and appliance dealers, home-improvement contractors and merchants of various kinds charged interest rates ranging anywhere from 25 to 75 percent and even more per annum.

The senators examined sample loan or "conditional sale" contracts printed in microscopic type that loaded staggering extra fees, charges, costs and penalties on top of regular interest charges.

But credit cheats do not limit their activities to consumers. There is a type of gyp that preys primarily on small and medium-sized businessmen who find themselves suddenly in need of cash. Members of this breed advance needed sums on short notice—and at astronomical rates of interest —taking the businessman's stock, accounts receivable or capital assets as collateral. If the borrower fails to meet his payments on the dot, so much the better. The sharpsters are eager to seize the collateral—invariably worth far more than the amount of the loan.

Bad as all this might seem, it is only one side of the story. Actually, there are very few people who really *need* to borrow or buy from credit sharks. Banks and legitimate lending institutions will lend money or finance purchases and charge only the legal rates of interest, adding no extras. Reputable dealers and merchants sell on credit and charge reasonable interest for this service.

Truly astute businessmen never try to make money on the interest they charge for making sales on credit or time-payment plans. They want to sell their goods or products and make their profits on the sales price, not on the interest charges, which they peg only as high as is necessary to meet the costs of handling a credit account.

After World War Two, the Spartan Aircraft Corporation reconverted to the peacetime production of mobile homes. I insisted that the interest rate on all time-payment purchases be held down to five percent, even though other firms were charging twice that. Spartan's sales boomed; the five-percent rate was ample to meet all the costs of credit selling. Soon other companies lowered their interest rates.

Many people do not take the time and effort necessary to shop around, to investigate carefully before they borrow or buy on credit, and all too often they fail to read what they sign. Many are still afraid of banks. Others are impatient; they want their shiny new automobile or the money they intend to borrow right now. They don't want to wait until the formalities attendant upon, say, a bank loan are completed. And, like some of the old-time wildcatters, they listen to the blandishments of the fast-talking credit gyps, who promise everything and deliver very little of what they promise.

Yes, there were many forms of frauds and swindles in the oil fields of Oklahoma. Not even experienced, cautious men were always able to avoid being cheated, and sometimes the situations that arose had their amusing aspects. I recall how one of the smartest and most successful among all independent oil operators once fell victim to a swindler's trick—and how he obtained his revenge.

The oilman is now dead and his name, though it was long a household word, doesn't really matter. I'll call him Fred Johnson, which is close enough.

Johnson was bilked in Oklahoma by a crook who sold him an oil lease at a sky-high price. There was a well on the property covered by the lease and, when Johnson inspected it before the deal was closed, the well gave every sign of being a producer. It was only after he'd paid over his money that he discovered he'd bought a dry hole that had been soldered up and filled with crude oil the swindler had trucked to the site.

The crook vanished, but Fred Johnson swore he'd even the score if it took him the rest of his life. Ten years later, in Texas, Johnson accidentally ran across the man who had cheated him. The gyp did not recognize his onetime victim, for Fred had gained weight and looked much different than he had the last time they had met.

Fred Johnson saw an opportunity to obtain his long-deferred revenge. As it happened, he'd brought in a dry hole on a property only a few weeks earlier. He now had his crew rig a hidden pipeline from an oil-storage tank to the dry well. After arranging to have himself "introduced" to the man who had swindled him, Johnson talked his way around to offering the crook the lease on the property in question. He said he'd sell it for $60,000—a low price, considering there was a "big producer" on the land. The swindler was interested, particularly since Johnson gave some plausible reason for wanting to sell out so cheaply.

Fred took the prospective buyer out to the site. Sure enough, the well was bringing up a steady flow of sweet, high-gravity crude—and the deal was closed on the spot. Fred Johnson collected the $60,000 he'd asked for and signed the necessary papers. That same day his men quietly dismantled the pipeline that had been feeding the crude oil to the dry well. The sharpster who had cheated Johnson ten years before now discovered that he had been repaid in full *and* in kind.

By no means can it be said that all oil swindles have involved only individuals who were actually in the oil industry. Through the years, uncounted tens of thousands of people have lost their life savings in swindles that were based on the sale of bogus stocks or shares in worthless or even non-existent oil leases. A prime example was the notorious C. C. Julian scandal, in which a corporation authorized to issue five million shares of stock actually issued fifteen million shares. A collapse was inevitable, and when it came, thousands of small investors suffered heavy losses.

Despite the clear warnings provided by such swindles, many people still persist in buying fake stocks and worthless leases. These are most generally sold by high-pressure promoters and gyps, almost all of whom have never even seen an oil well at close hand. They capitalize on the glamour of the oil industry and on the facts and legends of the fortunes that have been made in it. They sell their beautifully engraved, but virtually meaningless, "certificates" through the mail or by using boiler-room telephone-sales techniques. Some individuals are unable to resist the glowing promises of huge profits and throw their money away under the mistaken impression that they are investing it.

Of course, stock swindles are not limited to oil stocks. Worthless shares of all kinds are peddled by opportunists and cheats. Highly dubious shares are touted by some individuals and firms who blandly designate themselves "investment advisors," but who are apparently in business for the sole purpose of encouraging the wildest and most dangerous forms of stock speculation.

"If you had followed our advice, you would have made $10,000 on a $2500 investment in the last 120 days. . . ."

"We will give you the names of 15 stocks that we expect to double in value during the coming month. . . ."

"Let me tell you how you can make $50,000 on the stock market in only six weeks. . . ."

Such are the advertisements and claims of these "investment advisors." These claims are at best misleading, for they are most often based on nothing more than beliefs or hunches, and the "advisors" never mention their wrong guesses. At worst, they are intended to set off frantic buying waves to line the pockets of the "advisors," who have bought the issues they recommend at rock-bottom prices for the express purpose of running up the prices and then selling out.

Even some mutual funds will take great pains to obscure the facts about their operations and financial condition. Not long ago, one such mutual fund went so far as to send out an annual report that conveniently made absolutely no mention of the fact that its assets had dwindled by no less than $49 million during the previous 12 months.

Instead of reading brochures and advertisements dreamed up by high-pressure promoters and gyps, prospective investors would be much better off if they memorized and heeded this warning from

Keith Funston, president of the New York Stock Exchange: "Some would-be investors are attempting to purchase shares of companies they cannot identify, whose products are unknown to them, and whose prospects, at best, are uncertain. Some people have not yet discovered that it is impossible to get something for nothing."

There is no real reason why anyone should allow himself to be cheated when he buys stocks or invests money. Any individual can easily protect himself against fraud and chicanery, if he will only make the effort to do so.

The Federal Securities and Exchange Commission and various other federal and state regulatory agencies exist for the sole purpose of safeguarding the investor's interests. Reputable stockbrokerage firms and investment counselors will cheerfully provide prospective investors with complete and unbiased information about stocks and the companies that issue them. Trade groups, the Better Business Bureau and other agencies and organizations stand ready to inform and advise the public and to protect it from gyps and cheats. Whether he has ten dollars or ten million dollars to invest in stocks, an individual needs only to follow the dictum "Before you invest, investigate."

The same holds true for those who would avoid being tricked or cheated in other ways. Take, for example, the perennial rackets employed by the gyps who prey on the nation's homeowners. Door-to-door sharpsters solicit "home-improvement," "landscaping," "exterminating," "weatherproofing" and similar contracts. They offer what appear to be irresistible bargains in everything from house painting to lawn seeding to interior decorating. They

159

produce cleverly worded and entirely deceptive contracts for the homeowner to sign. If he does sign, he eventually finds that he has obligated himself to pay staggering prices for shoddy materials and grossly substandard workmanship.

Each year, the victims of these rackets are counted in the tens of thousands; estimates of their losses run into the tens of millions. Yet it is totally unnecessary for even one person to be bilked by these racketeers. The preventive measures are almost childishly simple: The homeowner should deal only with established, reputable merchants and contractors who, being part of the community, have a reputation to maintain. Then, of course, the homeowner needs only to contact the nearest office of the Better Business Bureau or his own chamber of commerce. These agencies will quickly provide him with all the information he needs about the glib salesmen who come to his door. Lastly, of course, no one should ever sign any contract or agreement unless he reads and understands it thoroughly beforehand.

Paradoxically, it's often more difficult for the businessman to protect himself against gyps than it is for the average individual. True, the businessman can also use the Better Business Bureau's services and there are credit associations that will provide him with information about the financial integrity and credit rating of firms and individuals. But there are highbinders who specialize in bilking businessmen. They're almost always experts at the fine art of financial juggling and chicanery. Because they're usually out to obtain large sums, they devise elaborate and convincing schemes to separate the businessman from his money.

A number of years ago, a wealthy industrialist I know was approached by two men who said they owned a valuable mining concession in South America. They produced deeds, documents and assay reports to substantiate their statements. Declaring they were in desperate need of funds to finance the exploitation of the property, they offered to sell him a 49-percent interest in the concession for $100,000, of which $25,000 had to be paid immediately.

All in all, the proposal seemed plausible and legitimate. The claims made by the men were believable and supported by apparently authentic documents. The references they gave checked out, and a telephone call to the South American bank they gave as reference verified their story.

The industrialist was about to agree and pay over $25,000 to bind the transaction. Then, at the last minute, he decided to hold off for a day or two while he made an independent investigation. It was fortunate for him that he did. The men were impostors: They had stolen or forged all their documents, including those that identified them as being whom they represented themselves to be. The actual owners of the concession were in the Middle East on a business trip.

Many other types of swindles are highly favored by crooks who specialize in mulcting businessmen. One popular form is the so-called nuisance suit. Nuisance suits are simply lawsuits filed on little or no grounds by individuals in hopes that the person or firm they are suing will settle out of court rather than spend the time and money and be exposed to the publicity attendant upon fighting the case in court. Trumped-up patent- or copyright-infringement suits, fake personal-injury claims and actions that dispute title to a property are typical examples of nuisance suits. The astute, experienced businessman knows better than to settle any such action out of court. He is well aware that it is nothing more than a form of blackmail. He always chooses to fight the suit; in the vast majority of instances, the plaintiff either drops the action or loses, because his case will seldom stand up in a court of law.

Bogus charity appeals are another favorite device used by swindlers. Every businessman and business firm receives hundreds of appeals from various charities each year. The requests for contributions are often made on expensive, embossed letterheads bearing the names of dozens of prominent persons who are listed as "patrons," "sponsors" or "committee members"—the implication, of course, being that if their names appear, the charity must be a deserving one.

Until comparatively recently, it was the custom of many firms to send contributions to all charities that appealed to them for funds. Then, as the number of appeals multiplied, it became impossible for even the largest companies to follow this policy. It also became apparent that some charitable organizations were badly administered and that some were even out-and-out frauds. In certain cases, the names of those shown as supporting or sponsoring the charity were used without the permission or knowledge of the persons concerned.

Thus, most businessmen today investigate all charity appeals with great care. They and their firms make contributions only to those that are known to be legitimate and that have been cleared by the Better Business Bureau or similar protective organizations.

By the same token, a businessman must exercise great care and caution before lending his name to groups or organizations that solicit him to serve on committees or to endorse them in any way. No matter how flattering such requests are to one's vanity, they must be investigated thoroughly. It is not unknown for an individual to endorse what he has been led to believe is a legitimate charitable, social, fraternal or service group only to learn too late that his name was being used by a fraudulent or even subversive organization. Needless to say, such errors—no matter how inadvertent and innocent—are liable to damage a businessman's reputation as well as his wallet.

It would be impossible for me to list all the unethical and illegal practices, tricks and swindles that either members of the public in general or businessmen in particular are liable to encounter. I have purposely omitted the categories of gyps sometimes found within business firms. Embezzlers, pilferers, expense-account cheats and the like are types against which any well-organized firm has built-in safeguards and which alert management automatically takes all necessary precautions to prevent.

Withal, neither the average individual nor the businessman has to worry much about gyps and swindles if he will only follow four simple rules:

1. No one should ever expect or try to get something for nothing. The mouths of gift horses should always be examined with meticulous care. There is generally something unsound or unsavory about any business proposition that promises tremendous

profits overnight. By the same token, although everyone loves a bargain, bargains are not always what they appear to be. Before buying, borrowing or investing, investigate thoroughly.

2. Deal *only* with established, reputable firms and individuals.

3. Never sign any contract, agreement or other document until you have read it carefully and are certain that you understand every word of it. If you have even the slightest doubt about what the paper you're signing says and implies, consult an attorney. You may be saving yourself a great deal of trouble *and* a great deal of money.

4. Lastly, and perhaps most importantly, be scrupulously honest yourself. It has been said that it's impossible to cheat an honest man by any form of swindle—that the swindler invariably appeals to the real or latent larcenous instincts of his victims. This is, of course, an overstatement, but it is certainly true that an honest man will scorn any dubious scheme, no matter how great the promised profits.

In short, the person who is himself open and honest and takes the time to examine all proposals made to him in the bright light of day will never fall prey to the gyps that pass in the night.

11.
THE MYTH OF A BALANCED FEDERAL BUDGET

A MASTER OF PROFITABLE ENTERPRISE DEFENDS UNCLE SAM'S RIGHT TO RUN IN THE RED

Tom Bailey's income before taxes in 1955 was $7500 per year. Only recently married, he owed $10,000 on his house and $1500 on his automobile and had other debts—for furniture, home appliances, and so on—totaling more than $3000. Yet no one—least of all Tom Bailey and his wife—considered him insolvent.

Today Tom's income has risen to $28,000 annually. He and his wife now have three children and, as could be expected, a much larger and finer house, two cars and a great many additional luxuries. They also have a much larger overall indebtedness. The unpaid balance on their new-home mortgage alone is more than $25,000, and there are sizable amounts due on the automobiles, the swimming pool in the backyard and their cozy summer place at the lake. Yet there are none—not even among Tom's creditors—who consider him a potential bankrupt because he hasn't paid cash for everything he's purchased and is deeply in debt. As a matter of fact, everyone who knows the Baileys and their financial situation considers them to be an entirely average family with what, under today's conditions, is an entirely normal financial balance sheet.

All of this would have little or no bearing on the subject at hand were it not that Tom Bailey is very active in community affairs and harbors hopes of someday running for public office. Personable, self-possessed and well spoken, he is frequently asked to address meetings of service clubs and businessmen's organizations in his suburban community.

Tom seldom fails to receive a rousing ovation after making one of his speeches—particularly one that deals with his favorite topic, the urgent need for balancing the federal budget.

"Years of government deficit spending have saddled not only those of us gathered here but our children and even generations yet unborn with a staggering debt," he declaims. "The trend must be stopped and reversed—immediately—if we are to have a healthy economy!"

It should be added that Bailey is an executive in a large corporation. Although he is a sales executive and thus not directly concerned with the company's finances, he conscientiously reads all the company's periodic financial reports. He is entirely aware that the corporation has large debenture issues outstanding and that it frequently borrows considerable sums for varying periods from banks and other lending institutions. But Tom isn't in the least worried. He sees, with great satisfaction, that the company's assets and liabilities balance out neatly, that there are ample reserves for contingencies; in short, he is sure that everything is in good order. He is certain of the company's future and its ability to meet all its obligations.

"Damn it! There's no reason on earth why the federal government can't be run the same way!" he snorts after studying one of his company's financial statements. "If private enterprise is able to keep its budget balanced, those people in Washington should be able to do it, too!"

How many Tom Baileys do *you* know?

I have met hundreds of them. Oddly enough, in many cases they are accountants and "financial experts"—the very men one would least expect to overlook the forest of obvious facts for the trees of baseless theory. They all ignore the same basic truth—that any attempt to compare the federal balance sheet to the balance sheet of a private individual or a corporation is akin to trying to compare an apple to an elephant.

The national debt—a red-ink bogey of approximately $361 billion resulting from years of federal deficit spending—is strictly a one-sided figure. It reflects *only* the government's cash-debt liabilities, while making no allowance for the nation's public-sector *assets*.

The fallacies inherent in this lopsided system of accounting have been pointed out succinctly by Howard J. Samuels, a former oil-company executive and undersecretary of commerce.

"The national debt is currently averaging some

$360 billion," Samuels observes. "Dividing by a population of about 200 million, we get liabilities of something approaching $2000 per person.

"At the same time, as good financial practice would recommend, we must also look at the assets of each American," Samuels continues. "Total assets in the public sector of this economy are somewhere around $2000 billion. To this should be added an estimated $750 billion worth of skills or human resources. If we then divide our $2750 billion in assets by the population, it turns out that the accumulated wealth of each individual is about $14,000. The differential of about $12,000 may well be considered the true financial position of every living American from the national point of view."

Can anyone imagine a corporation that owes, say, ten million dollars but that also owns assets worth seven or eight times that amount issuing a financial statement that reflects *only* its debts? Yet this is precisely what the U.S. Treasury Department does when it issues a report on budget deficits and the national debt.

My remarks should not be construed as a criticism of the federal accounting system. The government could hardly list every post-office building and national park—or every acre of federal property—as an asset. Nor can it show its aircraft carriers, atomic submarines, artillery battalions or guided missiles as capital investments and depreciate them on an annual basis. But, a dissertation on the peculiarities and paradoxes of government accounting systems could be continued indefinitely, and it would still lead to the same conclusion: The federal government simply is not "in business" in the same sense as General Motors or, for that matter, Joe's Diner. (Of course, there was a time when governments *did* show profits—when nations were ruled by monarchs whose principal purpose was to enrich their personal treasuries.)

And, conversely, my argument should not be interpreted as a defense of governmental waste. I firmly believe that the government must exercise every possible economy consistent with its aims, responsibilities and obligations. Such economies make particularly good sense in an inflationary period such as the present. But powerful social and economic pressures, wars hot and cold and the problems posed by population explosion, automation and countless other factors make it extremely difficult for even the most conscientiously frugal administration to balance the budget year after year with the stroke of a presidential pen.

At first glance, the layman might think it a relatively simple matter to slash sizable sums from an annual federal budget that ran close to $180 billion in fiscal 1968. It would, on the face of things, seem even simpler if one recalled that only 41 years ago—in 1930—the total of all federal appropriations was under $3.5 billion, about a fiftieth of what it is now. (In 1930, the War Department—including both the army and the air corps—had appropriations totaling $465 million. Today, with defense appropriations in the neighborhood of $80 *billion*, the Pentagon allotted close to $7 billion last year just for the purchase and maintenance of land vehicles.)

Statistics are dull. Nonetheless, I feel it necessary to cite some here. According to the U.S. Treasury Department, the gross national debt in 1950 amounted to approximately $257 billion. By the end of 1968, this figure had risen to $361 billion. This represents an increase of $104 billion, or an annual increase of nearly $6 billion.

So far, so good—or bad, depending on how you wish to look at these basic figures. But what happened to *private* debt during the same period?

In 1950, private debt in the United States totaled nearly $251 billion, roughly $6 billion less than the gross national debt. By the end of 1968, private debt had soared to nearly $1104 billion: Private debt had more than quadrupled, rising at an average yearly rate of about $47 billion. Of the 1950 private-debt figure, $142 billion was represented by corporate debt. In 1968, this corporate-debt figure stood at $586 billion, an increase of $444 billion for the period and, parenthetically, considerably greater than the gross national debt.

Finally, let us look at the figures for America's gross national product. The 1950 GNP was $284.6 billion. Reports for 1968 show that the GNP had nearly trebled in the interim, rocketing to more than $851 billion.

Note that for 1968, the total private debt was more than three times the gross national debt. Note, also, the corporate debt for that year—$225 billion more than the gross national debt.

Obviously, our economy is fueled by credit, which is just another way of saying that it runs on and continues to expand on one form or another of deficit spending. Property of all kinds is purchased, expansion programs are implemented, additional funds are obtained, emergencies are met— all through credit, by confidently banking on the future.

What some people fail to take into consideration is that the federal government must also expand—buying more things, financing more projects, obtaining, and providing, more services. Whether one agrees with what the federal government does in this, that or another area of its multitudinous activities is not the question. Ours is a democratic form of government. Our leaders are chosen by the majority and, presumably, the laws they pass and the policies they establish are in accord with the will of the majority. If they are not, there are democratic procedures for changing the leadership.

In the past few decades, the government has assumed—or has been forced to assume—a myriad of tasks and responsibilities. It has moved into areas of activity that were previously matters of concern solely for private enterprise. This has, of course, caused much criticism from certain quarters. Loud, indeed, have been the howls about government encroachment and creeping—or galloping—socialism.

I do not feel that everything the government does is always right and good. However, I have lived long enough and am enough of a realist to understand that government policies have, in general, served to improve living conditions for all, to strengthen the economy and to ensure our security.

Some of the most strident critics of our growing national debt are often the first to grab at government subsidies or to fight for government orders. When the government spends money on anything that is not of direct benefit to these individuals or to their own business interests, they characterize the expenditures as pork-barrel spending and politically inspired waste. But when they or their enterprises stand a chance to benefit financially, they are the first in line, eager to take full advantage of whatever the government has to offer.

To reiterate, the federal budget and the national debt are, in a manner of speaking, purely accounting fictions. The former is purely a *cash* budget, while the latter is a cumulative cash debt. No balance sheet or report concerning either ever reflects the immense assets—tangible and intangible—that the nation possesses to offset its deficits and debts. Suppose the federal balance sheet reflected the true value of every government building, of every acre of ground owned by the government. What would happen if a conservative allowance were made for goodwill, at home and abroad? How much is the Smithsonian worth, or a naval shipyard?

A company makes huge capital investments in plants and equipment that are intended to produce goods or provide services on a commercial basis. They are to be sold, presumably at a profit. The federal government's capital investments are in national highways, battleships, ICBMs, stockpiles of strategic materials and innumerable similar projects and hardware that do not return a dollars-and-cents profit to the government. They can and do, however, provide benefits, safety and security to every American citizen, even to those who groan most loudly and most consistently about federal spending.

I have been a businessman all my adult life. I have a strong and abiding faith in American business and its demonstrated ability to work miracles. Nevertheless, I can hardly imagine any business firm or combination of giant corporations volunteering to undertake the building and maintenance of all the nation's highways. I can't picture any privately owned company establishing and maintaining the nation's armed forces, taking them over from the government and showing a profit at the end of the year.

There are always cries about the continuing deficits shown by the United States Post Office Department. But let a legislator introduce a bill that would raise postal rates and put the Post Office on a self-sufficient basis and an outcry is raised by all the private enterprises that would suffer from such an increase.

We might as well face the issue squarely: A balanced government budget is not nearly so important as a safe and sound nation. Deficits do not mean disaster for a nation that possesses gargantuan tangible and intangible resources and assets justifying its deficits and serving as security for its debts.

The Tom Baileys and their companies have faith in themselves, in their ability to retire their debts in the future. They count on continuing growth and expansion of their incomes and profits to create economic strength. But when it comes to the question of government spending, they cling to the magical myth of the eternally balanced budget as the panacea for all the nation's real and imagined ills.

Is it that they have less faith in their country than they have in themselves?

This is a very good question—one that every American should ask himself the next time he goes into a flap about the bogey of the unbalanced federal budget. It is a question especially pertinent at the present time, when, despite all the complaints about federal deficits, the United States is enjoying the greatest prosperity in her history.

Uncle Sam's budget may not be balanced, but the economy of the United States is healthier than it has ever been and shows every sign of growing stronger in the future. This fundamental fact, which should be obvious to all, should also be enough to make a mockery of the myth of a balanced federal budget.

12.
MILESTONES
OF
SUCCESS

**THOSE CRITICAL DECISIONS
THAT DETERMINE THE COURSE
AND THE PROGRESS
OF EXECUTIVE CAREERS**

There isn't a human being who can be right about all things at all times, and this is at least as true of businessmen as it is of bartenders, biologists or bus drivers. On the other hand, there are times when a businessman makes what prove to be exactly the right decisions and takes what are precisely the proper courses of action in certain situations. It is at these times that he achieves the major successes that form the milestones in his business career.

My own first big success stemmed from the purchase of the Nancy Taylor Allotment Lease in Oklahoma in 1915. Although I realized only some $12,000 profit after drilling my first producing well on the property and then selling the lease, this initial triumph had a very important effect on my life. Several factors involved in the Nancy Taylor Allotment episode served to determine the course my business career would thenceforth follow.

First, I had originally bought the lease from under the noses of older, more experienced oilmen, and this gave me the confidence I needed in my own judgment and basic business ability. Then, having drilled a well and struck oil, I gained confidence in my abilities as an independent oil operator. Last, but far from least, the exhilaration I derived from this initial success was enough to convince me that I would never be content working anywhere but in the oil business.

I can recall other notable milestone successes during my wildcatting days. In 1921 the California Oil Rush was reaching new peak levels. Notwithstanding a break in crude-oil prices earlier in the year, the petroleum industry was rapidly getting back to normal, and by fall the fever to open new producing fields in southern California had once more reached epidemic proportions.

My father and I were contemplating a joint exploration and drilling venture in southern California, but we hadn't yet made up our minds exactly where to begin our "prospecting" operations. In October 1921, a new field was opened up in the Santa Fe Springs area south of Los Angeles. During the first days of November, my father and I decided to drive down to Santa Fe Springs to see for ourselves whether the region held any further promise.

Wanting to have the best of expert advice, we retained a highly regarded geologist to accompany us. I drove the car, and when we reached the area, we rode around slowly, all three of us carefully eyeing the topography of the land. The geologist wasn't very enthusiastic about what he saw.

"I'd say there were much better possibilities elsewhere in southern California," he declared dourly as we drove along Telegraph Avenue. "This doesn't look like very promising oil land to me."

A few moments later, we saw a long freight train laboring across what appeared to be a level expanse until it reached the crossing at Telegraph Avenue. After that, it began to gather momentum; although the locomotive's power eased off, the train steadily picked up speed. Clearly, there was a slight gradient—imperceptible to the eye—that had its summit at Telegraph Avenue. The implications of this struck both my father and me at the same moment.

"Did you see that?" my father demanded, a note of excitement creeping into his voice.

"I'll say I did!" I exclaimed.

"This is oil land—I'm sure of it!" father declared. "The top of the structure—the dome—is right here along Telegraph Avenue!"

I nodded my agreement enthusiastically, and even our companion, the geologist, had to admit that we had probably made a valuable discovery.

On November 21, 1921, my father and I bought the Nordstrom Lease covering four lots located right on Telegraph Avenue in Santa Fe Springs. We spudded our first well on the property a short time later, and it came in early the following year to produce 2300 barrels daily.

The real value of the discovery, we'd made while watching the freight train chuff its way past the Telegraph Avenue crossing became apparent soon enough. The Nordstrom Lease property proved to be extremely rich in oil, and we drilled

180

additional wells, all of which proved to be excellent producers. In the 15 years between 1922 and 1937, the wells we drilled on the Nordstrom Lease sites showed a total excess recovery—a total clear profit —of $6,387,946!

The Athens Lease was another turning-point success for me. I bought the lease in 1924—on my own account—paying about $12,000 for it. The lease covered a property located in what were then the southern suburbs of the city of Los Angeles— on Hoover Street between 127th and 128th streets.

Other operators were already drilling in the area, but they were going after oil in the deep zone. After taking a careful look at the drilling operations then under way, I became convinced that greater production could be obtained at considerably less expense if one drilled for oil in the upper zone, and went ahead with my own operations accordingly, personally supervising the drilling.

I completed my first Athens Lease well on February 16, 1925, and it yielded 1500 barrels daily. Three weeks later, I spudded my second well and brought it in within six days for an initial daily yield of 2000 barrels. The two wells were to show an excess recovery of over $400,000, and other operators promptly began to alter their drilling programs to go after the oil I had proved existed in abundance in the upper zone.

A year later I was offered the Cleaver Lease in Alamitos Heights by a man who had bought it less than a week earlier. I knew the property and felt certain that there was oil on it.

"How much do you want for the lease?" I asked.

"I paid four thousand dollars, and I'm satisfied to double my money," came the reply. I didn't argue—not for a single moment.

"You've just made a sale," I grinned, taking out my personal checkbook and writing a check for $8000.

The four wells I drilled on the Cleaver Lease property brought in almost $800,000 in clear profit during the next 12 years.

These and other fortuitous lease purchases and drilling operations were all important successes during the period when I was just a wildcatting operator. A truly major triumph of an entirely different sort was my successful campaign to gain control of the Tide Water Associated Oil Company —a campaign that began in March 1932 and did not end in final victory until almost 20 years later.

There is, of course, a vast difference between buying an oil lease and drilling a well and setting out to buy a controlling interest in a major oil company. Tide Water Associated was an old, established American firm. It had been founded in 1878 as the Tide Water Pipe Company to build and operate a then-revolutionary 104-mile-long pipeline for transporting oil from Titusville to Williamsport in Pennsylvania. In the decades that followed, the company grew into one of the American petroleum industry's giants. By 1932 it was among the 12 or 15 largest oil companies in the United States.

Tide Water Associated was big business, and its incumbent directors and management personnel were big businessmen with a great deal of experience and with huge financial resources behind them. By sharp contrast, I was nothing more than a comparatively insignificant upstart wildcatting oil operator.

Nonetheless, I made what proved to be the right

decisions and—with the invaluable assistance and advice of my aides and associates—took the right steps at the right times. It was a long, difficult fight, but in the end I won it. Much of the credit for the victory belongs to the men who remained fiercely loyal and confident even when the outlook was so bleak that it appeared virtually hopeless.

The late David Hecht, my brilliant and tireless attorney, guided the myriad operations involved through labyrinthine legal mazes. E. F. Hutton and Company brokers Gordon Crary, Ruloff Cutten and Don Phillips worked miracles for me with their adroit handling of stock transactions on the New York Stock Exchange. Emil Kluth and Harold Rowland were only two among many who gave me moral and material support when such support was needed most. Without the help of these men, the campaign that resulted in my biggest single business triumph might well have ended as my biggest and most dismal business failure.

The success of my companies' operations in the Middle East has been another important milestone in my business career. There, again, it was necessary to make the right decisions and follow the correct course of action, and the allowable margin for error was slim, indeed.

Admittedly, by the time I embarked on the Middle Eastern venture, I was a seasoned businessman. Even so, it was a giant step into what, for me, were relatively uncharted fields, and the problems involved were proportionately as formidable as any I had encountered previously during my business career.

In short, what I sought was a concession to drill for oil in the neutral zone, a largely barren desert area lying between the kingdom of Saudi Arabia and the sheikdom of Kuwait on the Persian Gulf —actually an arbitrarily defined geographical area owned jointly by the two states.

In 1948, two half concessions—one Kuwaiti, the other Saudi Arabian—became available. Another firm—formed by a consortium of oil companies—obtained the half that was the sheik of Kuwait's to grant. There remained the other half—the 50-percent concession controlled by His Majesty, King Ibn Saud of Saudi Arabia.

My initial decision to enter into the bidding for this latter half was influenced in no small part by the highly favorable reports on the region that were made by Dr. Paul Walton and Emil Kluth, outstanding geologists associated with my companies. They concurred in the opinion that tremendous quantities of oil lay beneath the trackless wasteland of the neutral zone and recommended that I take the multimillion-dollar gamble necessary to obtain the concession and begin prospecting and drilling operations.

"In the Name of God, the Merciful and Compassionate, this agreement is entered into in Riyadh on the 22nd day of the month of Rabia II, in the year 1368, corresponding to the 20th day of February, 1949. . . ." Thus reads the opening line of the voluminous agreement that my representative, Barney Hadfield, signed when negotiations for the concession had been successfully concluded.

The agreement granted me a 60-year concession on a half interest in neutral-zone oil. In consideration, I made an immediate cash payment of $12.5 million, but this was only the beginning. I would spend a total of considerably more than three times that amount before the first barrel of crude oil was brought in.

Now, the half interest granted me by the king of Saudi Arabia was, like the half granted to the other company by the sheik of Kuwait, an undivided half—an indivisible share. In other words, although two companies had been granted separate concessions by the rulers of two different states having cocontrol over the neutral zone, the companies were required to share equally in oil discovered and produced by either. In this way, Saudi Arabia and Kuwait would each receive revenues and royalties according to the terms of their respective concession agreements, but based on equal quantities of oil.

It would hardly seem necessary to point out that this arrangement posed many knotty problems —some of which occasionally grew to the proportions of major dilemmas. For example, the company that had obtained its half-interest concession from the sheik of Kuwait had its own ideas about prospecting and drilling for oil in the neutral zone. These views did not coincide with those shared by my associates and me, with the inevitable result that a great deal of time that could have been devoted to finding and producing oil was spent in negotiation and controversy over who was to do what where, when and how.

I wanted to drill in a certain region, but the other firm's experts insisted on starting drilling operations in another spot some miles away. I capitulated, and a great deal of time—some four years in all—and fantastic sums of money were spent in futile operations.

Eventually, however, it came our team's turn

to call the shots. In 1953 we discovered one field which by 1957 was producing nearly nine million barrels annually. In 1955 we located another field and drilled two wells which were producing at an annual rate of some two million barrels by the following year.

Then, in 1957, having obtained a considerable degree of autonomy in regard to our oil-prospecting operations, we really hit our stride. We quickly discovered several additional new fields and drilled many more wells, boosting neutral-zone production into the tens of millions of barrels annually. Another success had been achieved, but the end is nowhere in sight. Independent geological surveys state that proven reserves in place in the area covered by my concession exceed 13.5 *billion* barrels!

My business career began when I struck oil on the Nancy Taylor Allotment in Oklahoma and realized a $12,000 profit after selling the lease on the property. I encountered many difficulties and experienced many disappointments in the years that followed. But I can chart the course of my career by such milestone successes as those I have described.

I think the same holds true for any successful businessman. His first notable success serves to give direction and impetus to his career in whatever field he enters. If he possesses the inclinations of the true business entrepreneur, he strives constantly to achieve progressively bigger successes. Wherever possible, he builds each new one on the foundations provided by those he has already achieved.

To the real entrepreneur, there is no such thing as an ultimate triumph. His aim is to make a continuing and overall success of his career, and he knows the only way this can be accomplished is by achieving a continuing series of successes.

The businessman who wants to reach the top can afford to be pleased when he manages to accomplish an end against the odds he inevitably faces. But he cannot afford to allow any of his achievements to make him complacent.

While the successful businessman recognizes his notable achievements for their importance, he regards them primarily as road markers that serve as invaluable aids in guiding the future course of his business operations and career.

In my own case, I firmly determined to stay in the oil business after my initial success with the Nancy Taylor Allotment Lease. Subsequent successes as a wildcatter provided me with additional experience, produced more profits that I could use as working capital to expand my operations and gave me more confidence in my business ability. Each of my milestone successes also served to whet my appetite for facing greater challenges.

By the time I started my campaign to gain control of the Tide Water Associated Oil Company, I felt that I had served a hard, instructive apprenticeship in the oil business. I had learned my oilman's trade from the bottom up.

I believed that I'd learned my lessons well. I wanted to apply my knowledge to projects of broader scope. I was convinced that by implementing ideas and plans I had formulated in the oil fields, I could direct the operations of Tide Water Associated more successfully than they were then being directed by the company's management.

I did, of course, eventually succeed in my campaign to gain control of Tide Water Associated, but only after a long, uphill fight against odds that look frightening even in retrospect, long after the battle was won. Yet I consider my victory only a minor achievement compared to the far more important and meaningful success my associates and I achieved in building up the company after I had gained control of it.

The assets of Tide Water Associated—later Tidewater Oil Company, now merged into the Getty Oil Company—multiplied until by 1965 they exceeded $800 million. Tidewater's operations have mushroomed in size and scope; it operates with greater efficiency and with greater benefit to stockholders, employees, customers and the public at large. Nevertheless, I do not consider even these achievements anywhere near final. In my opinion, the company still has far to go.

My attitudes toward the operations of Getty interests in the Middle East conform to similar patterns. Obtaining the neutral-zone concession, locating the area's vast oil deposits and eventually attaining high levels of oil production there are all achievements that can be considered milestone successes in my career. But the job in our Middle East oil fields is far from finished. There is room there, too, for expansion and improvement—room for more and bigger successes.

I believe that to be truly successful, the businessman must first discard—or, at the very least, greatly discount—most traditional concepts of success. And he should critically examine whatever preconceived theories he may have about gauging or achieving it.

Let me reiterate my contention that there is no such thing as the ultimate success in any business that operates under a competitive, free-enterprise system. Nor is there any such thing as success that is inherently lasting, that will not fade unless it is nurtured.

There is nothing constant about business. The business world is a changing one; the business scene varies from day to day and even from hour to hour. Thus, no single achievement will long retain its initial value. The startling success of today can soon become obsolete and worthless—the abject failure of tomorrow.

I learned early in my career that an oil well that came in for, say, 2000 barrels a day initial production could run dry long before the costs of drilling it had been recovered.

By the same token, a manufacturer may put a revolutionary new product on the market one week only to have a competitor introduce an even more revolutionary one the next. A sales campaign that is sweeping the market can be buried by the avalanche of another that proves to be more effective. The programs introduced by a company president may achieve great success for a time and then be wrecked overnight by developments over which neither he nor anyone in the company has any control.

Success is at best fleeting. The only way in which a businessman can hope to achieve anything remotely approaching lasting success is by striving constantly for success in everything he attempts.

In this, a rough analogy can be drawn between the businessman and the motion-picture or stage star. A relatively unknown actor may be catapulted to stardom because of a part he plays in a single production. Overnight, he becomes a popular idol, and he is swamped with offers from producers. But what happens if his next role is a bad one or if the next production in which he appears is a flop? His popularity wanes rapidly. Unless the roles he plays and the productions in which he plays them immediately after his setback are successful, the star will find that he has become a has-been.

Intelligent theatrical personalities—those who have remained on top year after year—are acutely aware of these perils. They examine all offers with extreme care, turning down roles they feel do not suit them, refusing to appear in productions that are below standard. When a theatrical big name does accept a role, he spares no effort to give the best performance he can.

Naturally, not *every* performance and *every* production can be an Academy Award winner or draw critical raves. There will be some of each that will be mediocre or even bad. But the top names are those whose average of hits is highest and who consistently do their utmost to do their best. It seems to me that to these extents the successful actor and the successful businessman have much in common.

The businessman who can build an entire career on a single success is a rare bird, indeed, if he exists at all. The businessman whose career can survive an unbroken series of failures after even the most remarkable of initial successes is rarer still.

To carry the analogy one or two steps further: The successful actor meticulously examines scripts offered to him. He learns all he can about the producer, director, the other actors proposed for various roles and the technical personnel with whom he will be working if he accepts the part offered to him. If he does accept, he rehearses endlessly—

and then gives the finest performance he possibly can.

A businessman reaches the top and stays there in much the same manner. He realizes that business successes are seldom coups, but, rather, the results of painstaking planning and hard work. The successful businessman examines any given business situation with at least as much attention and care as the successful actor examines his scripts. Usually, the businessman will be even more painstaking, for he must concern himself with such added dimensions as costs and competition, production rates and profits and other such matters not normally within the actor's province.

The businessman also concerns himself with people—the personnel with whom he has to work as well as those with whom he is dealing or intends to deal. Then he plans carefully, going over his plans again and again, searching for flaws, seeking ways to improve or better them, and this is the businessman's version of the actor's rehearsals. When at last the plans are ready and it is time for him to act—in the broad sense of the word, of course—the businessman, like the actor, gives the finest performance he possibly can.

No matter how well things turn out, the seasoned businessman knows that he cannot stand indefinitely taking bows and acknowledging the applause. If he wants to stay in business, he must do something for an encore—and the sooner the better. When the late, great John Barrymore achieved his first huge successes as a star of the legitimate theater, he was once asked what he thought about while taking his opening-night curtain calls.

"I think about two things," Barrymore is said to have replied. "First of all, I think about improv-

191

ing my next performance so that I'll get more curtain calls. Then I think about what part I'd like to play after the show finally closes."

It may be true that there's no business like show business, but everyday businessmen could do far worse than to use a paraphrased version of John Barrymore's answer as their guide. Once a business success has been achieved, the astute businessman gives thought to amplifying his achievement, and he is immediately alert to opportunities that may grow out of it or to new opportunities that may present themselves.

Sooner or later, every businessman has his big opportunities to achieve big successes. He must be able to recognize them when they present themselves, and he must also possess imagination, ability and willingness to work hard—the elements needed to make the most of his opportunities. These are not necessarily innate traits or abilities. In most instances, businessmen acquire and develop them as they go along.

But once he's recognized his opportunity and set his sights on a goal, the businessman must lay his plans with great care. He must handpick the aides and associates in whom he reposes the greatest confidence—individuals he can inspire to devote their utmost energies to the tasks he has set for them, just as he must exert his own energies to the utmost.

If he does these things, he will greatly enhance his chances of achieving a milestone success. After a while, it will become almost a habit, and a series of milestones will mark the path of a long and truly successful business career.